Sacred Trees,
Sacred People
of the
Pacific Northwest

ॐ

Sharon McCann

Library and Archives Canada Cataloguing in Publication

McCann, Sharon, author
    Sacred trees, sacred people of the Pacific Northwest / Sharon McCann.

Issued in print and electronic formats.
ISBN 978-1-5331-3593-3 (softcover).--ISBN 978-0-9958452-0-6 (HTML)

    1. Nature--Effect of human beings on--Northwest, Pacific. 2. Human
ecology--Northwest, Pacific. 3. Trees--Northwest, Pacific. 4. Northwest,
Pacific--History, Local. 5. Northwest, Pacific--Biography. I. Title.

GF504.N87M33 2017   333.7'09795   C2017-900025-X
                                                    C2017-900026-8

&

DEDICATION

I dedicate this book to my husband Richard Hart, spiritual
ecologist, biophysical monitoring pioneer, Pacific Northwest
naturalist, dedicated teacher, and much more.
Thanks to your connections, insight, knowledge of the
Pacific Northwest, and constant love and faith in me,
I completed this journey.

I also dedicate this book to John, Renee and Leila Mae,
Honour, and Cat because you inherit our world.

CONTENTS

ACKNOWLEDGMENTS

In Gratitude

I bow deeply in respect to all the persons represented in this book who gave me their time and trust. Thank you friends who read my chapters and gave me feedback: Richard Hart, Deb Whitall, Robert McDowell, Dana Gerhardt, Terre, David Edgar, Julie Fox, Marie Gaudreau, Mona Saunderson, and Ian Douglas and his writers group. Thank you Periodical Writers of Canada and Mark Zuehlke for funding and mentoring. Thank you Charlotte Gill and Richard Therrien for your editorial expertise.

Permissions

Prologue

David Suzuki and Sarah Ellis, excerpt from Salmon Forest. Copyright 2003 by The David Suzuki Foundation and Greystone Books. Reprinted by permission of The David Suzuki Foundation and Douglas & McIntyre Ltd.

David McCloskey, excerpt from "On Bioregional Boundaries," in Raise the Stakes Vol. 14, Winter 1988/89. Reprinted by permission from the publisher Planet Drum Foundation, PO Box 31251/San Francisco, CA 94131, Shasta Biogregion. Email mail@planetdrum.org.

Jean McLaren, excerpt from Spirits Rising. Copyright 1994 by Jean McLaren. Reprinted by permission.

Chapter Three

Arlene Jensen, excerpt from Clan Chronicles. Reprinted by permission from Carol Jensen.

Chapter Four

Arthur Lee Jacobson, excerpt from Trees of Seattle, Second Edition. Copyright 2006 Arthur Lee Jacobson. Reprinted by permission.

Chapter Six

Cascadia Forest Defenders, excerpt from Anti-oppression policy, www.forestdefenders.org. Reprinted by permission.

Cascadia Forest Defenders, excerpt from "Expleted Deleted," midwinter 1999, reprinted fall 2002 edition, Green Canopy. Reprinted by permission.

Chapter Eight
Loraine Robbins, excerpts from Journal from Down Under, Bravenet, 2005. Reprinted by permission.

Chapter Ten
Alan Sasha Lithman and Ashland Daily Tidings, excerpt from Guest Forum, "The City cut down more than a tree," Ashland Daily Tidings, July 2, 2001. Reprinted by permission.

Chapter Eleven
W-FIVE, CTV Television Inc., quotes from W-FIVE segment "Singing Trees," January 24, 1995. Reprinted by permission.

Chapter Twelve
Bill Jackson, "The Wall" published by the Redwood Record. Reprinted by permission of the publisher.

Meaveen O'Connor, "Grounding and Growing the Force of Compassion." Reprinted by permission.

Photo Credits
Chapters Two, Nine, Eleven
Julia Butterfly on top of Luna, Shrine in Luna's cave; Jerry Franklin in his grove; Singing Forest clearcut, and Glada McIntyre: photos by Richard Hart. Reprinted by permission.

Chapter Seven
Cheewhat Giant Cedar photo by Angie Bailey, 1989. Reprinted by permission.

Chapter Ten
Ashland Ginkgo tree photo by Terry Skibby. Reprinted by permission.

8❧

PROLOGUE

Because I am rootless, I admire the rooted. The rooted stay in one place. The rooted are connected to family and neighbours, to town and city, to province and state. The rooted put down their roots and branch out, being nurtured by the place that supports them.

I grew up among the concrete and highways of Southern California. My mother had left her Connecticut roots behind to relocate to the golden land of two seasons, liberal culture and beautiful beaches. When my parents divorced, my mother and I relocated from apartment to apartment. I felt like a sapling transplanted over and over again, whose tender roots repeatedly broke. Before the age of maturity I took to the road, which I knew well. Along the way, I studied trees, mostly the way they were uprooted and stuck in places they didn't belong, to scar the horizons as telephone poles. I too was a misfit.

After immigrating to Canada, I grew fond of the native maples gracing the sidewalks of Montreal. They spoke of the seasons—all four of them. I liked the season of falling leaves the best because of the many shades of red, yellow and brown maple leaves. I loved their playful whirling in the wind, and their raked piles so fun for my children to jump in. But the value of those trees were, to my awareness at the time, mostly ornamental. When I moved to British Columbia (BC) in 1994, I met trees. The grandeur of the evergreens commanded my awe. The more I hiked among the mountains of Southern Vancouver Island, the more I noticed the trees dancing and singing, just like Emily Carr had painted them.

During an interview for my first job in Victoria as a publications editor, a professor with long hair slapped down on his kitchen table a coffee-table book with the title: *CLEARCUT*. This was the cause of his

1

organization, he explained. Ecoforestry Institute had an important mission—to protect and sustain whole forests. As I flipped through the book that put Western civilization to shame I was stunned. I had no knowledge of where our lumber came from or how it was extracted. The photos revealed former vast forests that were now many heaps of tangled slash and stumps strewn over the hills, mountains and valleys of North America, looking like amputated arms and legs left behind from military conquest. The subtitle of the book read "The Tragedy of Industrial Forestry."

I sympathized with the mission and was hired. I started work in the basement of a home of another sympathizer. It took several months to get established in a real office in downtown Victoria. My job was to manage a newsletter and journal for the Institute. There we stayed—a variable staff and a family of mice—until we could no longer pay the bills.

During this sojourn of about a year, I learned about forestry through the eyes of famous forest stewards. I followed behind the likes of Merv Wilkinson, who claimed to have logged his 55.03 hectares (136 acres) on Vancouver Island for 50 years without depleting the forest of its original board feet. I listened to Herb Hammond explain the erosive effects of clearcutting on the land and on the heart ("What does it feel like?" he would ask of us. I realized I didn't know and had never paused to notice). I asked bold questions that amused the students of environmental studies ("What's a snag?" Answer with a polite smile: "A dead standing tree"). I scribbled in wet notebooks as we slogged through logged forests in the rain. I learned about highgrading (logging the best trees and leaving the least merchantable). I watched woodlot owners perform increment boring to measure the age of a tree. I went to lectures by ecologists and followed them on tree walks. I met forest stewards from all walks of life—university trained foresters, untrained inheritors of forested land, biologists, citizens engaged in forest conservation, and loggers who loved the land and wanted to leave forests behind for the next generation to log.

After that immersion in tree society, I went on to other jobs in other places. But a view that had been expressed by the tree lovers I had met— that trees are sentient—continued to linger in my psyche. When I heard it spoken, I often snickered—privately. Trees were alive, I agreed; but they didn't feel or communicate, I reasoned. At the same time, I wondered. And the more I entered woods and forests to renew myself, the more I paused to notice what I felt.

I became more curious about this region that felt more and more like home. Borders of the Pacific Northwest, I discovered, depend upon your vantage point. I found motel postcards in Oregon that claimed Oregon,

Washington and Alaska for the region. I checked the *Atlas of the Pacific Northwest*, which defined the place as Idaho, Oregon and Washington. *The Arbutus/Madrone Files,* written by Canadian author Laurie Ricou, defined the regional boundary by the native range of arbutus (so called by Canadians, or madrone to Americans), which extends from the east side of Vancouver Island at the latitude of Desolation Sound, down the coast of the island and mainland BC to San Luis Obispo County, California. In *The Nine Nations of North America* published in 1981, American author Joel Garreau distinguished the wet Pacific Northwest coast, which he called "Ecotopia" (inspired from the book *Ecotopia*), from "The Empty Quarter." Ecotopia ranged from Point Conception (south of San Luis Obispo) to the Kenai Peninsula of Alaska. The Empty Quarter—or the bulk of BC, Alaska, northwest Canada and US western states—contrasted with Ecotopia by its higher and drier status, richness in energy resources, unpopulated ranges, and cowboy culture. Ecotopia, claimed the author, was populated by open-minded people who were enriched by high tech and aerospace industries and angered by nuclear power plants, pesticides and clearcutting.

When I asked Canadians about the Pacific Northwest as a region, those who recognized the term said that it's an American perspective, since the Yukon is BC's northwest. And yet, British Columbians do recognize their province as part of the Cascadian bioregion that includes BC, Washington and Oregon. In 1999, the Cascadia Mayors Council claimed the region to be the tenth largest economy in the world if ranked as a nation-state.

The name Cascadia comes from the Cascade mountain range that starts just north of the international border in BC and ends with Mt. Lassen in northern California. The Scottish botanist David Douglas named the range during his explorations of the Pacific Northwest. Perhaps the name was inspired by the cascading waterfalls of the Columbia River as it passes through a gorge to the Pacific Ocean. Beginning in the foothills of the Canadian Rockies, the river flows through BC and Washington and separates Washington from Oregon as it slices the Cascades east to west on its 1953-km (1214-mi.) journey.

West of the Cascades in Washington, Oregon and California are more Coast Ranges that block the westerly winds moistened by the Pacific Ocean and trap the rainfall that grows the great evergreen conifers, able to photosynthesize year-long due to mild winters. Even the mountains and river valleys of the Columbia Plateau, which lies east of the Cascades, collect enough rain to grow tall pines, hemlocks, spruces, firs, and cedars. The plateau offers diversity to the monotony of Pacific Northwest rainforest, growing grass and sagebrush on the flat lands and hills between its mountains and valleys.

South of the plateau and east of the Cascades, the Klamath River begins to flow and empties into the Pacific Ocean in northern California where rain falls in abundance again upon the coast redwoods. From the fog belt of these redwoods to Kodiak Island in Alaska stretch about one half of the world's remaining coastal temperate rainforests—a scarce and unique bioregion worldwide. In BC, the provincial term for it is the coastal western hemlock zone. Further afield in BC, western Oregon, and Washington, the Douglas-fir, hemlock, and true fir forests grow.

Another species common to the forested watersheds of the Pacific Northwest is salmon. By the time the Spanish and British began to explore the northwest coast in the late 18th century, the First People had learned how to fish, preserve and protect the salmon they depended on. Salmon once teemed in both the Fraser and Columbia Rivers and their tributaries. (The Fraser River emerges from the Canadian Rockies and travels 1400 km [636 mi.] to the Salish Sea. The Columbia River basin traverses BC, Washington, Oregon, Montana and Idaho.) In the children's book, *Salmon Forest,* authors David Suzuki and Sarah Ellis described the connection between salmon and forests this way:

[Daddy says] "All the poop from the bears, eagles, otters, ravens, coyotes, and other animals that eat salmon helps the forest grow." [Daughter to Daddy] "When we eat salmon we're like the bears and bugs and trees, right? It's like we're salmon humans."

Cascadia Institute founder David McCloskey defined Cascadia north and south by the rivers where salmon run, and east by the Continental Divide that runs along the ridge-top of the Rockies. His definition of Cascadia includes the southeast edge of Alaska, most of BC, Oregon, and Idaho, all of Washington, parts of Northern California (as far southwest as the Russian River), Montana and Wyoming, and little pieces of Nevada and Utah. McCloskey drew the southern-most border of Cascadia around Cape Mendocino and the Mattole River. For 15 years he explored Cascadia, trekking over 128,747 km (80,000 mi.) by car and foot to find its natural boundaries. During one of his walk-abouts he climbed onto a Washington mountain peak and beheld the US-Canadian border. To his disgust he saw a 6-metre (20-foot) wide, straight-line clearcut running up and down steep slopes, and remarked that such an arbitrary political line is what bioregionalists abhor: "Surely the winds aloft and the fires in the earth below, as well as the trees, birds, salmon, and native peoples, do not acknowledge such arbitrary boundary lines as significant."

In my perusal of Pacific Northwest literature, I identified a current of thought that flowed through the region like its rivers, gaining influence over time. In the 1975 novel *Ecotopia*, author Ernest Callenbach described an ecological utopia in which people collectively agreed to let the forests sustain life. Ecotopia was an imaginary future nation of two-

and-a-half states (Washington, Oregon and Northern California) that seceded from the union, with San Francisco as its capital. In the story, a journalist who visits the nation years after secession falls in love with an Ecotopian, and chooses to remain in ecological utopia powered by solar energy and small-scale, appropriate technology, where the work week is short, forests are not clearcut, and people talk to trees. After reading the book I contacted the author. Did he talk to trees? I asked. Mostly he told me how a collective of his friends published the first edition of the book in Berkeley, California, and that it sold 23,000 copies. Then Bantam bought the paperback rights, after which the book was translated in nine languages and sold almost a million copies. Ernest claimed it was influential in founding the Green Party in Germany.

I followed a similar thread in the 1985 book *Deep Ecology*, that also rallied for ecological utopia. *Deep Ecology* authors Bill Devall and George Sessions, both northern Californian college professors, collected the thoughts of Norwegian ecologist Arne Naess, ecofeminist Carolyn Merchant, northern California poet Gary Snyder, and others to synthesize the basic principles of a democracy for the biosphere: that humans and non-humans—including bugs, rivers, rocks, forests, and trees—have equal rights to flourish.

The sentiment that trees are sentient continued to spread. In 1990, Redwood Summer (named after the 1960s Civil Rights campaign, Mississippi Summer) campaigned for the civil rights of redwoods. Roused by EarthFirst! leaders Judi Bari and Darryl Cherney, demonstrators marched through northern California timber towns to block logging of the redwoods. While on tour to enlist support for the protest, Judi and Darryl were injured by a car bomb that blasted nails into Judi's pelvis and lower back, instantly paralysing her. FBI agents and Oakland police arrested her (on a hospital bed 12 hours later) and Darryl Cherney for possessing explosives. Bari and Cherney sued FBI agents and Oakland police for false arrest, illegal search of their homes to find evidence of bomb making, and slander in the media that portrayed them as terrorists. Over a decade later, the ashes of Bari, who died of breast cancer in 1997, sat in the courtroom where the verdict was read. In 2002 the jury unanimously ordered the FBI and Oakland police to pay $4.4 million in damages to the estate of Judi Bari and Darryl Cherney for violation of their rights to free speech and protection from unlawful searches. The notion of sentient trees had become fraught with risk and danger.

Three years after Redwood Summer, in the summer of 1993, an estimated 12,000 Canadians, Americans, Europeans and Australians travelled to Vancouver Island to protest the BC government's decision to log much of the largest intact temperate rainforest remaining on

Vancouver Island—Clayoquot Sound. The arrest of 856 adults and children who blocked the logging trucks in Clayoquot Sound led to the largest mass trial in Canadian history. "What many people who read the media reports did not realize," protestor Jean McLaren told me, "was that while some days only two or three people were actually arrested, there were often more than two hundred supporters on hand." As grandmothers were removed in leg shackles from the blockades, songs and poems were sung by those who said no to the clearcutting. Like drums beating, words pulsated from the hearts of people united. This song was sung to the tune of "Amazing Grace":

> Amazing place oh Clayoquot Sound
> Where grows a forest so free
> With soil, and fern and branches high
> Let life so sacred be. . . .

Within a few years of living in the Pacific Northwest, I realized that the place had changed me, simply because I longed to be in the presence of trees, especially the ancients who sway when a strong breeze sighs in their upper reaches. I began to wonder if the trees were calling to me, in some nearly imperceptible way of course, and that I was nearly hearing them.

So like the big tree hunters of North America, I became a hunter of sentient trees. In 1998 I began to journey into parts of the Pacific Northwest within my reach, that is, BC, Washington, Oregon and Northern California. I looked for relationships between people and trees, for that would indicate communication or sentience. I found trees that became catalysts for personal and community change, so I called the trees sacred. I found people who seemed to be ordained by the trees, so I called the people sacred too. And throughout my journeys I privately hoped that perhaps one day, I too would be able to communicate with trees. But I didn't know why it mattered, until the end.

⧸❦

Chapter One
THE ASKIN' ROCK TREE
Stein River Valley, British Columbia

Afloat on a narrow reach of the Fraser River, I wasn't sure where this ferry would lead me. Of course I knew where I was, having driven 160 km (99 mi.) northeast from Vancouver through Lytton, formerly the ancestral village of the Lytton Band. The indigenous men who hand-operated this two-car ferry were brown like the waters of the Fraser. They came from here. Their ancestors lived and died here, and their stories connected them to this place. I came from where I had last lived, never knowing about the ancestors of that place.

When I arrived on the other side of the river, I drove onto West Side Road into a First Nations reserve. I drove up to a two-story grey house. Before it grew a garden of many colours and a green lawn, which seemed out of place because the landscape was dry. At the same time, the greenery suggested care and attention, which relieved me. I parked behind the house where Ponderosa pines stood straight up from bare dry ground.

Within minutes, a good-looking, heavy-duty pick-up truck drove up. A native hopped out, followed by wife and child. A baseball cap topped his long curly hair tied behind his back. He extended a hand and smiled with his eyes, in perfect semi-circles. "Welcome," said Terry, shaking my hand. "I was waitin' for you all day but didn't know for sure if you'd come."

I had indeed taken my time. Months earlier, I found Terry's name in a hiking book about the Stein. This 1060-sq km (409-sq. mi.) river valley surrounded by mountains contains one of the largest rock art sites in Canada. In the distant past it was common for youth of the Nlaka'pamux and Lil'wat Nations (Lytton and Mt. Currie Bands) to enter the Stein. Vision questing empowered them to take their place in service of the tribe. The visions of the questers were recorded in red iron oxide on the rocks. After two centuries of colonial imposition and two generations of residential schooling, vision quests had nearly died with the rest of native culture. For two decades, the First Nations resisted logging threats to their valley. Allied with environmental campaigns that drew thousands of supporters, they succeeded. In 1995, the province declared the Stein River Valley a heritage park.

In the 1980s and 90s, Terry served his people in the Rediscovery program, helping native youth get in touch with themselves in the wilderness. I found his telephone number by calling directory assistance, and dialed. When Terry answered, I said I was looking for a sacred tree. "Everything in the Stein is sacred," he replied. He said he led vision quests for anyone interested, and got calls from people all over the world. It took me awhile to commit to a solitary fast in the wilderness among cougars and grizzly bears.

Twelve hours after my arrival at this portal to the sacred, I awoke to the call of my name. It was dawn and my head throbbed from a night of drinking herbal tea in a buffalo horn, sweating in a home-made lodge perfumed by Saskatoon berry leaves, and cooling down in the water of an old white bathtub on the lawn, all the while blessing our relations. I had crashed in my tent on the lawn—a luxury compared to what my accommodations would be for the next three days.

"Time to go," said Terry, kneeling outside my tent. He had to go to work after dropping me off in the Stein. Terry had two jobs. One was a day job that paid the bills, and the other was appointed by the tribal elders.

We drove a short distance and parked in the dusty lot of the Stein trailhead. I lumbered out of the truck and hoisted a large pack on my back.

"What d'you bring in that?" Terry asked, half-smiling. He was toting a small canvas handbag.

"Just a change of clothes for four days and a camera," I said. I didn't admit the first aid kit, knife, rain gear, and small propane burner for boiling water.

"The Stein River is sweet and clean," he said. "You don't need to boil the water."

I half-smiled in disbelief; the Stein Valley BC Parks brochure advised boiling all water. With a caffeine withdrawal headache already brewing, and the prospect of no food for days, I was tempted to say that I preferred the water boiled and caffeinated, but I didn't.

Terry led and I followed into the park. The path was well worn and I imagined his ancestors entering with us to quest. Perhaps others are using the place even now, I thought. Would I have company? As we walked, I felt bold and cautious at the same time. I listened to the rushing river parallel to the trail and noticed the large Ponderosa pines on the slope beside us. The trees exposed their thick, serpent-like roots above the ground. Bunchgrasses, knapweed and kinnikinnick sprang up wherever they could take hold. Everything looked thirsty. In the old days, I had read, questers chewed the tops of firs to quench their thirst. In the old days, they slept on fir boughs. I looked forward to sleeping on my air mattress.

In about 20 minutes we reached a cliff wall beside the footpath. Terry stopped and I gawked, looking upward at its unusual formation. Carved out of the upper half of the wall was a shelf that was wide and long enough for a body to lay down. It was thought, I had read, that the feet of shamans had created basins such as these during their questing. Below the shelf, in the cracks and hollows of the cliff face were stuffed tobacco, sage bundles, cigarettes, painted stones, shells, coins, beads, bracelets, and even a cigarette. Terry said it's tradition for people to pray at the cliff upon entering the Stein. He called it the Askin' Rock.

"Make your offering," he said. "Whatever you ask for, ask for the details. Like if you want a car, ask for air conditionin'." It was 6 am in July, and already I felt waves of heat. At this time of year near Lytton, it was really hot. At the time, Lytton held the record for the second hottest location in Canada, at 44.4° C (111.9° F).

I pulled out my Redman's tobacco—slightly blushing about the brand—and stuffed some into a crack. Then I looked up to the sky to pray, but in the way of sky and prayer was a tree hanging horizontally over the cliff.

I just looked at it. It was short, with stumpy, lichen-coated branches that reached out into space like claws. Perhaps it was a Doug-fir, but I could see no needles or cones to know for sure. Terry motioned to move on. We quickened our pace onto a thin trail that led us upward along the side of the cliff.

Above the Askin' Rock was a flat top. We sat down on it in full view of the mountain side opposite us. Below rushed the Stein River, green-blue and white-capped. Near our feet and issuing from a crack in the rock was a very weathered tap root. I leaned slightly forward to observe the rest of the tree hanging over the cliff. Terry said, "My wife an' I got married beneath 'er. Start'd a tradition in the community. Maybe she'll leave us next winter. Then we'll have a ceremony an' burn 'er."

Terry paused to recollect. I contemplated a tree that would get last rites.

Askin'
Rock
Tree

"My wife an' I hung bundles on 'er branches once. When we came back they were gone." Terry seemed surprised. I thought, You're not suggesting this tree is some kind of spirit post, are you? But I didn't say anything, or even make a skeptical face. I just leaned over again to look at the Askin' Rock tree, marvelling at its emergence from rock.

Terry took some tobacco and a pipe from his tote and we smoked. Then we got up and turned to face the mountainside behind us. The immediate surroundings were open, with shrubs and trees here and there. The place looked wild and tended at the same time; some spots appeared flattened as though people or animals had laid there. Terry said to find my power spot.

As I walked about, my legs shook like a newborn deer. Without any attention to location, I unfurled my air mattress and plopped down with a thud. Terry made up for my lack of ceremony and took out a bundle of sage from his supplies. He pinched some leaves and sprinkled the herb around my power spot. "Bears never cross sage circles," he said.

If only it were that easy, I thought. I imagined cans of sage lining the shelves of outdoor stores in place of pepper sprays. And then I saw former fields of sage clearcut from Lytton to Vancouver. No, far better to keep this remedy to ourselves, I said to myself.

"I can sure make use of sage," I replied to Terry. I hoped it would repel cougars too.

He handed me the herb bundle. Then he passed me a small plastic bag of dried roots. "Chew on this an' keep it under your tongue. It'll keep you from cravin' food an' help the visions to come."

༄

Chapter Two
LUNA
Humboldt County, California

Within a year of my vision quest, I read about a young woman who had perched within an old-growth redwood in Northern California. She committed to not set foot on ground until the tree was saved from logging. Her name was Julia Butterfly. From her platform in the branches, she spoke to the world at large through her cell phone. She addressed rallies, conferences, festivals, summer camps, and churches. She gave interviews for print, radio and TV, including a live debate on CNN with the president of Pacific Lumber Company. To support her treesit, Julia founded a non-profit organization called the Circle of Life Foundation.

Like members of the media, I called her directly to request a visit. She welcomed me to visit but said I would not be able to ascend the tree to meet her face to face. That privilege would be reserved for two financial supporters of the treesit.

By the time I went to see her, Julia had been treesitting for one year and seven months. It was August 1999 when we drove to Arcata, California. The plan was to meet Julia's ground support in town, who would lead us to the treesit. The group of us numbered five, including my husband Richard.

At 9 a.m. on a warm Saturday morning with clear blue skies, I knocked on the apartment door of our guide and woke him up. From behind the door, he said to wait in the parking lot while he got dressed and gathered gear. Soon he appeared at our cars, carrying ropes and packs. He was friendly and very fit, with large cautious eyes and shoulder-length brown hair. He introduced himself as Rising Ground.

While packing climbing gear into the trunk of one of the cars, Rising Ground explained his role. This hike to Luna would be number 63, he said, but he had done many more hikes on his own. Sometimes if Julia's cell phone broke down or she needed emergency supplies, he would hitch a ride and trek in and out of the forest twice a day. His job included coaching reporters up and down the tree on ropes. If they froze from fear of heights, he got them down. His name seemed to fit his role.

Before leaving town, we drove to the local natural food coop to buy donations of fresh food for Julia. Rising Ground said she preferred to eat raw food most of the time. Reserves of dried food were also stored on platforms in the tree, in case bad weather or a security siege cut her off from ground support.

After purchasing supplies, we headed south on Highway 101, passing Pacific Lumber Company's mill on the banks of the Eel River. Pacific Lumber Company owned the forest land on which Julia camped. For over a century, Pacific Lumber owned 220,000 acres (89,030.8 ha) in the heart of coast redwood land. It had built the town of Scotia to house its employees to maintain lumber production. The *Sequoia sempervirens*, or coast redwood, is the tallest tree in the world and highly valued for its knot-free, straight-grained wood. Although redwoods were said to regrow like weeds, the company modestly logged and selectively cut its forests. After Maxxam Corporation bought the company, Pacific Lumber was cited several hundred times for violating timber-harvesting rules of the California State Forest Practice Act.

We drove to Stafford and parked. The town sat at the base of mountainous land owned by Pacific Lumber. Rising Ground led us into the woods and upward on a well-worn footpath. He hiked quickly and took the rises in elevation with ease. When we stopped to rest, I asked if he was an EarthFirst!er, knowing that members of this group adopt forest names. He was not, he said, nor was Julia. She had been nicknamed Butterfly in her youth.

I had read that it was EarthFirst!ers who started the treesit in 1997. They had moved into the old growth redwood to protect it from logging and to protest Pacific Lumber's logging practices. They called themselves the Lunatics and named the tree Luna. In her lofty red branches with fine needle foliage they rigged a platform. Among those taking turns in the treesitting was Julia Butterfly. When treesitters went home for the Christmas holidays, she relieved them. At the time, she had no plan to persevere until Luna was saved; this experience was to be a stopover in her travels. She had recently donned a backpack at the age of 23 and left Arkansas to find her life's purpose. Just before that, she had suffered a head injury in a car accident and spent a year recovering.

During her first winter in Luna, Julia's resolve to stay put was tested.

She held on for life as branches snapped from 90 mile-an-hour (144.8 km/h) El Nino winds. Sleet and hail shredded the tarps sheltering her platform while she wrapped herself in tarps like a burrito. There was more to endure: a hovering helicopter blasting gusts of wind; security guards blowing bugles and air horns all night; and loggers threatening to cut down the tree with her in it. EarthFirst!ers wanted her to come down but she persisted.

Rising Ground led us onward and upward until he stopped at the top of a slope that had slumped. He seized the moment, being media-savvy:

"What you see here," he said, "is the mudslide that happened January 1st, 1997. Pacific Lumber put in a road incorrectly and they clear-cut this entire hillside, which is way too steep and unstable to be clear-cut anyway. When the whole hillside came down, a resident down below heard what was happening—Mike O'Neal heard trees snapping like they were bulldozed, and it had been raining for several days. He ran outside and got his daughter and ran to the neighbours and warned them of the mud. They evacuated. He saw this wave of debris, 20-feet high with stumps floating on top of it, coming toward Stafford. Seven homes got completely destroyed and several more got severely damaged."

I looked down the mountainside and saw how the slide of debris had gouged it. Over two years later, shrubs here and there had begun to reclaim a barren slope. I shuddered as I imagined the terror of facing a tsunami of mud and tree roots rushing toward my home.

We continued along the top edge of the slump, stepping gingerly while looking down. I looked beyond into the valley, noticing the Eel River curve northward, with the mill of Pacific Lumber sprawling on her bank. Rising Ground led us into the forest on a thin, worn trail. Soon I could see a blue tarp in the crown of a tree. Deep laughter cascaded like a waterfall. I could see Julia waving through dense foliage, 180 feet above ground, her arm swaying like a branch of white flesh.

The five of us reached the foot of Luna in a staggered way, each saying hello as we arrived, and then each of us becoming speechless. It's normal to greet your host, but it's not normal for her to be in a tree. Julia peered down as we congregated below. I could see her crescent-moon smile shining through the branches.

From her 4 x 7-foot (1.2 m x 2.1-m) platform, Julia started chatting with Rising Ground about matters of daily routine. She had dropped a small tape recorder to the forest floor, she said, and asked Rising Ground to find it. She wanted to tape the threats of a local who had come to visit a few days earlier; he had hacked at the underbrush and hung a crystal transmitter nearby to communicate with aliens. Julia dropped an empty pack by rope for the supplies we carried. Rising Ground told us she didn't need bottles of water— she collected water herself from the ever-present rain and fog.

As Julia chatted with the others, I looked at Luna. I followed my gaze around the huge trunk, noticing the charred bark. Coast redwoods survive forest fires admirably well, even though fire might carve passageways through their thick and fibrous trunks. Luna had suffered the same fate. As I walked around the tree, I discovered first one cave and then another, each cave being nearly halfway around. On the charred bark of one cave, a tree and heart had been carved. Inside the other cave, on the ground, sat two unframed water-coloured drawings of a butterfly and a Buddhist goddess. I recalled that redwood hollows were also sacred to the indigenous Chilula people, who had once settled along Redwood Creek east of Humboldt Bay. The Chilula claimed their ancestors came from the hollow of a large redwood tree. I looked into the darkness of the cave; it whispered of mystery and hinted of lurking spiders.

I walked back to the other cave where the others were standing. My gaze followed the massive trunk upwards. Way above my head a big burl poked outward from the trunk. From where I stood, it looked to be at least 5 feet (1.5 m) in diameter, but it could have been much wider. A rope dropped down the trunk, passing the burl. Julia and Rising Ground strategized about the ascents of our two companions.

Shrine in Luna's cave

Rising Ground showed the couple, one at a time, how to hitch-up to the seat and shoulder straps and pull up on the rope. It took about 20 minutes for each one to ascend to the lower platform in the tree, where Julia greeted them with laughter.

Rising Ground passed me a walkie-talkie. "You're not going to ask about how she shits in the tree, are you?" he said, slicing me with his eyes. This question must have been popular with reporters, I assumed. I shook my head no, even though it had been one of my questions. Instead, I asked: "What's it like to spend so much time with a tree?"

"As far as my interactions with Luna go," replied Julia, "that's what you hear when I speak. Luna is constantly communicating with me. And it's not all the time that I've interacted with her on a very intense, one-on-one level, like when I almost died in the storms. For the most part, Luna communicates with me just by the fact that we've basically become one together and I'm helping to keep her alive and she's helping to keep me alive. She communicates a lot with me every day, although not oftentimes in a way that makes me stop and go, 'Oh wow, that's Luna, that's amazing.' It's more of a constant flow of communication."

I detected an accent in her words, but couldn't put a place to it. She sounded like she came from everywhere. I knew she was the daughter of an itinerant preacher, and spent her childhood travelling with her family across the United States in a 31-foot (9.4-m) mobile home. When she entered high school in Jonesboro, Arkansas, her family moved into a house.

She continued: "What I've learned up here is that everything in life communicates. All of life communicates. We're all part of the same source. The wind has things to tell us, the rain, the birds, the plants, the animals, Luna—everything communicates with us every single day, all day long. The shift starts to happen when we start taking the time and have the desire to open up and to listen, and to truly listen and to hear what it is they're communicating to us."

She had the time to listen. By now, she had been sitting in Luna for about 20 months. "What else did you learn up there," I asked. She was quick to respond:

"I learned love on a level that no human being could ever teach me. I learned love on a level that no one can ever take away from me. And through that love, I learned the power of letting go. Because for unconditional love—that source-of-life love—you can't have attachments in order for it to flow in and out in this beautiful magical circle of life. And so the things like the frostbite, and the storms and the helicopters, and all those things taught me the power of letting go—letting go of comfort-ability, letting go of fear, letting go of anger. I guess the lesson began when they started cutting down all those trees, the ones you see on the ground down below. They cut them all down while I was here. Witnessing them destroying this grove for hours every day was like witnessing my family being killed. My reaction was to want to strike out. I begin to cry every time I think about it because I feel it to the very depths of my being. Everything inside of me wanted to strike out at those people, strike out at the violence to stop the violence. But I knew that there was something higher. That I didn't have to stoop to their level, that I could go to a higher source, and that source is love. And what that has taught me about myself is an understanding that, as long as we hold that life source of love in our hearts, our abilities and our possibilities as human beings are as boundless as this creation we're a part of."

I heard someone crying in the background through Julia's walkie-talkie. I looked at Richard; a few tears dropped down his cheeks. No one spoke for several minutes. I returned the walkie-talkie to Rising Ground. He began to busy himself with grounds keeping. Both Richard and I wandered about, finding stumps to sit on and reflect.

Julia Butterfly
on top
of Luna

After the couple descended, Rising Ground suggested we hike to the ridge above Luna to watch Julia climb to the tree top. We ascended to the top of the ridge to a landing for logging. Julia climbed to the top of Luna in bare feet with so much ease that it seemed as though Luna lifted her up with loving arms.

Unknown to any of us at the time of our visit, Julia and Pacific Lumber had begun to negotiate a deal. A few months after our August visit, they signed an agreement in December 1999: In exchange for $50,000 and Julia's descent, Pacific Lumber promised to protect the tree and a 200-foot (60.9-m) buffer in perpetuity. A local land trust organization called Sanctuary Forest agreed to be trustee of the conservation easement. While some treesitters thought that Julia gave in to corporate greed, the exchange of money was in fact the traditional path of redwood conservation. In the 1920s, Save-the-Redwoods League, and most notably the Humboldt Women's Save-the-Redwoods League, pursued Pacific Lumber until it sold some of its redwood groves for Humboldt Redwoods State Park. Soon after Julia set foot on ground, having lived in Luna for 2 years and 8 days, she began to fundraise to pay for the terms of protection.

Julia had been nicknamed "Joan of Arc of the redwoods" by the media, and nearly a year after her descent from Luna, the nickname proved apt. Sometime in late November 2000, around American Thanksgiving, a vandal slashed into Luna's trunk. The director of Save-the-Redwoods League called upon Dennis Yniguez to help. Dennis was an arborist from Berkeley, California, and president of the American Society of Consulting Arborists. Dennis told me the following story by telephone.

The very next morning, Dennis met with people at Pacific Lumber Company headquarters. The people came from California Department of Forestry, Pacific Lumber and Sanctuary Forest. They decided that the first thing to do was determine the extent of the damage. Everyone climbed into Pacific Lumber's four-wheel drives.

"We went up there with graph paper and tape and different measuring devices, accompanied by a few media reps," Dennis said. "We determined that over 60 percent of the cross-section had been severed. We could actually see Luna slightly rocking in about a 10-mile (16-km) an hour breeze. It was spooky. Luna was really slashed—the degree of penetration was 32 inches (81 cm). Somebody had stood inside the uphill fire scar of Luna and plunged that saw right into the heart of her, slashed both ways and then walked around both sides of Luna and extended the cut as far as they could."

With the extent of damages determined, the team returned to headquarters. They designed thick T-shaped braces made of half-inch plate steel with very strong welds to be screwed into the trunk. Bolts an inch thick attached to rods, which connected the braces above and below the saw cut. These bolts would be adjustable to hold Luna tight, since she would sway in the wind and storms.

"We had to design braces that took into account the physics of having a huge lever, 200-feet (61-m) high with a wind sail at the top, leveraging against the bottom of the tree. That's a lot of pressure," said Dennis. "I've never seen or heard of anyone doing braces like this to hold up a tree, so we really winged it."

They expected a storm that night. Pacific Lumber put several machinists overtime on the job. In two and a half hours, they fabricated five sets of two-piece braces, and packed trucks with a generator, hundreds of feet of electrical cord, night lights, a power drill, an impact driver, and wrenches. Dennis hiked in to Luna to guide by flashlight the vehicle convoy, which parked on the landing above Luna.

"We worked from about 7:30 at night until 11:45 solid," said Dennis. "And we worked frantically to get the braces on because we expected the storm. At 11:45 we started to pack up some of the tools, and just about midnight this huge storm broke. There were torrential rains and very strong winds, and nobody knew if Luna was going to make it through the night."

That night, Julia returned to California from Florida, where she had been visiting her grandparents. In the morning, a Pacific Lumber truck escorted her to Luna, passing new clearcuts on the way.

Minutes before a press conference in Eureka, Dennis arrived. "There were a lot of media trucks and cameras set up," he said. "Eric Goldsmith, executive director of Sanctuary Forest, came running out of the conference with open arms and hugged me. 'Luna made it,' he said. 'She's standing, she's standing!'"

Eric had spoken earlier with employees at Pacific Lumber about what had happened. They were unhappy about Luna being cut, they told him. He believed that what drove their sympathy was having a high regard for the law and legal agreements. Even though they might not have agreed with what Julia Butterfly did, even though they might have thought that Luna would be better off sawed into planks for a deck, they felt it was wrong to break the law and vandalize the protected tree.

Eight months later I drove down Highway 101 to visit Luna. Shortly before turning off highway onto the Stafford exit, I could see Luna's spire peaking above the other trees on the mountainside. I parked and waited for the Sanctuary Forest conservation easement monitor. Stuart arrived shortly before Ed, who drove up in a Pacific Lumber truck.

Luna's braces

Ed was the company compliance officer, and he was reserved and clean-shaven. Stuart was the easement monitor, and he was relaxed and bearded. Their roles were opposite too: Ed's job was to ensure that Pacific Lumber cut down trees according to the rules of the California Department of Forestry; Stuart volunteered to keep Luna standing in the centre of her easement. According to Julia's organization, the Circle of Life Foundation, Stuart was Luna's guardian angel. Lately he had been checking on Luna once a month. The first week after the tree was slashed, Stuart volunteered 50 to 70 hours.

I watched Ed and Stuart from a short distance as they talked man to man, long enough for both to lean onto Ed's truck. This was a unique relationship cultivated over time for the singular purpose of keeping one tree standing. When Ed left, I hopped into Stuart's truck and we drove slowly up the mountainside, with permission of Pacific Lumber. By driving instead of hiking, we got a better view of the clear-cuts. Stuart savoured his memories of the Stafford rallies in support of the treesit and the mass hikes to Julia and Luna. "That was my first taste," he said.

We drove as close as we could to Luna and parked on the logging road. To hike in to Luna, we passed above the slope of the Stafford mudslide. Willows had been planted here and there to hold the soil in place. By now, Maxxam had settled out of court with 26 Stafford residents, and paid them $3.3 million for damages from the mudslide.

Passing above the slump, Stuart let me go first. I hiked the same thin trail into the forest I had followed before, until I glimpsed the massive trunk of Luna. Drawing nearer, I could see the rip of the chainsaw cut. The cut extended around her trunk as far as a chainsaw could be brandished by someone standing on the upper slope.

Reaching Luna's base, we stood in silence. It was a natural thing to do before an old-growth tree that was born perhaps before Jesus Christ, or at least before Mohammed. We walked around the tree. The seamless nature of the cut spoke volumes about the effort to keep her standing. I saw no wide, jagged laceration—just a thin slit filled in with clay. Inside one cave butterfly and astronaut stickers beautified the bolts and braces. Inside the other cave we found feathers, bells, crystals, a Buddha pendant attached to a dream-catcher, a bundle of feathers left by Julia, a lock of dark brown hair, and a button that said "Your silence does not protect you."

"My favourite is the pink eraser," said Stuart as we stood looking at the offerings. "All I can guess is somebody badly wanted to leave something." Perhaps prayers were supporting Luna too.

Stuart inspected the bolts in the steel plates in the tree, since Luna's sway could loosen them. Months after the cut, three half-inch logging cables were anchored into the trunks of three redwoods on the slope above Luna to hold her steady. A fourth cable was anchored into the ground, 27 feet (8.2 m) deep. Five wraps of cable around Luna's trunk at 100 feet (30.5 m) formed a loose collar for the ground cables to be attached. Turnbuckles at the base of the cables could be adjusted to keep the lines taut.

"While we worked on the cables," said Stuart, sitting down beside Luna, "I got phone calls from biologists, chemists, and foresters telling me about different grafting techniques, polymers and resins to fill up the cut. Julia finally said she wanted to use something from the earth. She wanted to use soil and she asked me to talk to a Cherokee Bear Medicine Man in Cambridge, Massachusetts." Stuart smiled. "We had some wonderful long talks. He explained that Native American medicine has used clay as a healing agent for a long time. He said the bacteria in the clay would fight disease-causing bacteria that could get into the cut. To make the story more interesting, he said even better than clay is bear saliva. I laughed. 'Well,' he said, 'I know bear saliva is hard to get. You could use dog saliva, that would work too. You can even use your own saliva.'"

Since bear saliva was the best, Stuart went to a sympathetic zoo, taking a piece of celery and peanut butter to visit the bear. In exchange for peanut butter, the bear left some saliva on the celery stick. Then Stuart and company hiked to Luna bringing bear saliva and also local clay from Salmon Creek, carried in natural materials—cotton pillow cases, glass and wooden vessels.

"Julia came with us that day wearing sandals and socks and it was snowing," Stuart continued. "By the time we got to the top, her feet were soaked and cold, so she put her gloves on her feet and went the rest of the day like that." Stuart took out an album from his backpack and showed me his photos. "We all spit into the clay. Steve Salzman, the engineer who volunteered his time and designed the cable system, brought not only his spit but also a little chunk from the Great Wall of China."

We savoured the international flavor of this event. Then Stuart said, "A couple months later the clay begins to crack. While I'm thinking about this, I come home one day and there's a message on my answering machine from the Cherokee Bear Medicine Man. I haven't talked with him in two months, and he says, 'I'm getting this beam from Luna that you need to go and repack the clay. You need to keep re-packing the clay on a regular basis.'"

We stood up to examine the clay in Luna's cut for dryness. Stuart took out a small blue bottle from his backpack. It was a tincture made from Luna's bark and needles. He walked around Luna to drop the tincture inside Luna's two caves. Then we scrambled halfway up the ridge above Luna to check the turnbuckles anchored in the trees. He peered at Luna's crown with binoculars, noting that only one small top branch was brown. Stuart would keep an eye on it, he said. Some predicted that Luna would die from her wound within two years.

We hiked up to the landing and walked down the logging road to the truck. Stuart recalled how Julia walked this same path after descending from her treesit. "She was barefoot," he said, "and her feet were cut and bloodied by the time she reached a vehicle at the end of the road." I picked up a sharp, triangular rock and fingered its edges, holding this nondescript piece of grey slate like a holy relic.

Arriving at trail's end, we found the gate closed, with Stuart's truck inside the gate. He called Ed on his cell phone and left a message. Then he popped a Julia Butterfly CD into his audio system, inviting me to listen while waiting for Ed to open the gate. But I wanted to go. I took down Stuart's cell phone number to check on him later in case Ed didn't show. I was less committed than Stuart to the conservation effort.

Sign
beside
Luna

Just as I reached my car on the other side, a Pacific Lumber truck drove up and Ed opened the gate. Then Stuart drove up and parked beside me. "I'm glad you're still here," he said, searching his truck. "I forgot to show you something." He took out a fine pen drawing protected in 9 x 12-inch (22.8 x 30.4-cm) clear plastic. "I found this on one of my hikes to Luna. It was wet, and I dried it out. It's a drawing and letter by Julia."

The fanciful rendering of "Father Wind" was appropriately titled before the wind blew it out of Julia's grasp while treesitting. Stuart beamed. "I told Julia I found it because it could be raffled for money," he said. "She thought about it and called me back to say I could keep it."

I recalled what Julia had learned from Luna, that you can't have attachments for love to flow in and out of the circle of life. I wondered what I would learn from trees.

&❧

Chapter Three
TREE KEEPERS
Oregon

On the last weekend of summer in 2003 when a brilliant blue sky lured us to the Oregon coast, Maynard Drawson and I competed with a stampede of Portland motorists heading west on Highway 26. I drove while Maynard enjoyed the scenery.

"There it is, there's the sign!" shouted Maynard. "Largest Sitka Spruce in the United States." I looked for the sign ahead and slowed down behind several cars ahead of us, preparing to turn. I followed the cars into the parking lot of Klootchy Creek Park.

"I been here a hundred times," said Maynard as we got out of the car, "and I never seen so many people visit." As vehicles continued to enter the lot, tires stirred up the gravel and filled the air with dust. I noticed a portly woman emerging from her car with a video camera.

"So where is it?" I asked as I turned to Maynard, but he had already walked ahead. I followed him to where he stopped to talk with a senior couple standing before a wooden walkway. As I approached, I overheard Maynard say, ". . . and I'm the one who found it." The couple glanced back and forth between Maynard's big "I love trees" button pinned to his shirt and his be-speckled face, beaming with enthusiasm. Did they believe him, I wondered. "If it weren't for the heritage tree program, we'd a lost a lot of Oregon history . . . ." he continued.

While Maynard talked, I read a sign nearby, beside the walkway. It read: "Circumference 56 feet (17.1 m), height 206 feet (62.8 m), age 750 years, dedicated 1997 by a heritage tree committee. The largest tree in Oregon and the largest Sitka spruce in the United States." I looked all the way down to the end of the walkway, where a very tall tree stood on a very small island of temperate rainforest surrounded by a raised platform.

Most people passed by the sign without reading it and headed toward the tree. "Big tree, huh?" said one. "Yeah, wonder how tall it is," said another.

I left Maynard talking and walked down the walkway to the platform. A tall man with a protruding belly approached the tree with a camera. He looked up at the gash likely caused by lightning spiralling down the trunk to a point about 50 feet (15 m) above us. "I'm surprised they let people in here with the tree being damaged like that," he said. "They should require insurance."

Maynard walked jauntily onto the platform, sprightly for his 70-plus years. He introduced himself to everyone gawking at the tree. Behind the trunk a family posed for a photo.

"I found it," repeated Maynard to a growing crowd. "They were loggin' in here for the war. They were after Sitka spruce for that plane they were buildin' for England. So the supervisor come by here and saw that tree and he told them to leave it. They were gonna cut it out." A few more people gathered around Maynard, who continued: "It had limbs all the way to the ground when he first got here. Now they've limbed it up. It's almost 60 feet (18.3 m) around, and it's the biggest Sitka spruce in the United States except for one out by Lake Quinault that they claim is bigger, but it was born on a nurse log, on a stump. When you measure 4.5 feet (1.4 m) up you're not even getting into the trunk—you're still in the root system. I let 'em recognize the one in Washington because nobody cares. But this is the biggest tree in Oregon."

By the end of the day, Maynard made some Oregonians proud. He had also invited so many people to lunch in Salem that he didn't know how he would pay for it.

At the next opportunity, I accepted Maynard's invite for a free lunch in Salem. He said to meet him at White's Restaurant on a Thursday, when you could order Maynard's meatloaf. Established in 1936, the restaurant was a Salem institution like Maynard, although Maynard was older.

Entering the vestibule of the diner, I spied several plaques on the wall near the front door. I read each one: "Oregon Heritage Tree Program, Maynard Drawson Founder. Presented by Oregon Heritage Tree Commission, Oct. 12, 2001"; "Oregon Community Trees and the Oregon Dept. of Forestry Recognize Maynard Drawson with the 2001 Oregon Urban and Community Forestry Lifetime Achievement Award for Outstanding Achievements and Contribution to Urban Forestry."

Maynard
and the
Sitka spruce

As I entered the dining area, I found Maynard sitting in the first booth by the door, greeting everyone coming and going. We shook hands and I sat down opposite him, behind the table. He continued to speak to customers. He appeared to host the lunches on Thursdays.

"Did you get enough to eat?" he asked an elderly woman. Her eyes lit up and Maynard twinkled.

"You come in here again," he said to another patron on the way out. "I'll have a different woman with me next time."

Uncomfortable with the implication, I quickly asked: "So Maynard, how did you get interested in big tree hunting?"

"I was interested in everythin'," he said. "I love fishin' and huntin' and trees and I got into the *American Forests* magazine. I noticed every couple years they'd come out with the largest tree of its kind in the United States. Well, I started readin' that and I was absolutely fascinated. So when I started writin' my books, I dedicated one chapter out of all the chapters in the book to the trees in Oregon, Washington and Idaho—the Northwest. And that's when I really got into the tree business."

As we ordered and ate lunch, Maynard explained how he self-published a series of five books titled *Treasures of the Oregon Country*. They recorded family outdoor adventures with his seven children and big tree hunting. With a large family and wife at home, he wrote his books between haircuts in his Salem barbershop, and got forewords from some of his clients, notably Governor Tom McCall and Senator Mark Hatfield. He would have written two more books, but quit after falling out of a tree on his 40-acre (16.2-ha) forest outside Salem.

Maynard continued: In 1973 he nominated the Oregon Sitka Spruce as a champion for the National Register of Big Trees, maintained by the conservation organization, American Forests. Thirteen years later, big tree hunter Robert Van Pelt discovered a Sitka spruce on Quinault Lake in Washington State and nominated it, claiming it to be the biggest Sitka spruce in the United States.

An impartial group of observers gathered to determine which tree should rightfully reign as champion in the National Register. Maynard and Robert tagged along with the party that travelled from Klootchy Creek Park to Olympic National Park in one rainy weekend, using the same equipment. An American Forests formula would determine the overall stature of the trees by a point system that adds the circumference (measured at 4.5 feet [1.4 m] above ground), height and average diameter of the live crown.

Measurements revealed the Oregon Sitka to be 56 feet 3 inches (17.2 m) around and 206 feet (62.8 m) tall, resulting in 856 points. The Washington Sitka measured 58 feet 11 inches (17.9 m) around and 191 feet (58.2 m) tall, for a total of 883 points. American Forests wisely decided to make the trees co-champions, even though official policy for co-champions requires two scores that fall within five points of each other.

Twenty years after nominating the Oregon Sitka spruce for the National Register, Maynard said he got a phone call from the logger who saved it. To Maynard, the call was a miracle. For 20 years he had been wanting to find out why the tree was saved, given that all the trees around it had been felled. The logger told him that it wasn't saved because it was a record tree. It was saved because it had limbs all the way to the ground. They wanted spruce trees that were straight, without knots. During both world wars the Pacific Northwest native Sitka was favoured for aircraft because the wood is exceptionally strong for its weight, able to absorb the damage of bullets and be repaired quickly. Many a Sitka spruce was logged—and many spruce forests depleted—to obtain boards with straight grain; an estimated one board foot in every 50 board feet qualified for airplanes.

Maynard said he made a date with the logger. They planned to meet at the tree with the Oregon Secretary of State to post signs on Highway 101 to direct motorists to the tree on Highway 26. As far as Maynard knew, that was the first time that signs were posted on a highway to a tree that wasn't on that highway. But Maynard never got to meet the logger; he died two days before the signs were posted. Maynard said that broke his heart.

I asked him why he cared so much about preserving trees. He said, "If we appreciate the world we live in, it will be a lot easier to protect it, and make it better for everybody. If everybody was just thinking of themselves, we'd have a pretty messed up world. As it is, it's getting messed up."

By 1997, Maynard had initiated four city and county heritage tree programs as well as nominated 11 National Register champions. He had been looking for an organization to adopt a state heritage tree program. At the time, American heritage tree programs were common to cities but not to states, although states kept big tree registries.

Maynard discovered the Oregon Travel Information Council, which managed the state's historical marker program and highway rest stops. He convinced the group that historical trees were a good fit for their program. In 1997, the Oregon Heritage Tree Program proclaimed its first heritage tree—the Klootchy Creek Sitka spruce. Undisputedly it was the first state heritage tree in the country.

Also in 1997, Arlene Munkres Jensen nominated the second state heritage tree. "This tree was part of an orchard set out by Salem pioneer Benjamin Franklin Munkers in 1850," Arlene wrote to the Heritage Tree Committee. "It originally shaded the family home. The Munkers' wagon train, composed entirely of family members, came to Oregon in 1846 and settled east of Salem."

Arlene was the great-great-great granddaughter of Ben. She had traced her family history to a man named Moncas who invented the monkey wrench in the 1700s. The name changed to Muncas, Munkres and Munkers, which Benjamin Franklin Munkers inherited. Ben left Missouri in April 1846 by wagon train. Along with 95 other wagons led by oxen, the Munkers set out with 10 children who needed five wagons because four of them were married. Ben's wife was so ill she could not walk, and made the entire journey on a feathered bed that sat atop her coffin. Ben was pragmatic. The pioneers had heard about the dangers of roving bands of wild Indians and thieves, so Ben kept $10,000 in gold and silver in the bottom of the coffin, guarded by his wife.

By early autumn the family reached the Columbia River, surviving an encounter with warring Indians, a hurricane and avoiding cholera that had killed other pioneers en route. They followed Barlow Pass on the Oregon Trail, and reached the green Willamette Valley by October. Ben bought a homestead of 640 acres (259 ha) at Mill Creek for $1000. Within ten years, an orchard produced a bounty of pears, apples, and peaches, and Mrs. Munkers outlived her husband.

The Munkers later sold a part of their homestead to the Hagers, who transformed the orchard into a popular picnic and camping grounds for Salem urbanites. Development continued until highways, residential streets, suburban homes, a golf course, and a shopping centre fragmented the old orchard, leaving a few remnant trees in a large field. The pear tree that Arlene nominated as a heritage tree had been named after the Hagers. It inspired her to write a song, sung to the tune of "Red River Valley" at a Munkres family reunion:

> . . . From Missouri it came as a seedling,
> Only one of a hundred or more,
>
> Carried west in an old covered wagon,
> Planted deep in the rich Valley floor.
>
> Where an orchard bloomed in 1850
> Traffic flows now in multiple lanes;
> The old homestead's now part of the city,
> But the tall, lonely pear tree remains. . . .

I asked Maynard how to find the Hager pear tree. He said there was no easy access, which I discovered. By exiting Interstate 5 onto Highway 22 heading east of Salem, I glimpsed a brown sign on a post standing behind a low highway railing. The sign read: "Hager Grove Pear." I couldn't slow down to admire the tree due to vehicles behind me. I wondered if drivers ever admired its display of abundant white blossoms in the spring.

Hagar Grove pear tree

I drove up and down Highway 22 several times, looking for a place to park on the same side of the highway as the tree. Finding a small mall near a fast food restaurant, I spied a parking lot. I turned left onto a street intersecting the highway, entered a driveway and followed it to the parking lot. I parked and stood outside my car to spot the tree. A chain link fence bordered the parking lot and the field where the tree stood. I walked to the fence, saw that it had been cut open, passed through the hole, and followed a worn footpath along a ditch below the highway.

As I approached the tree, I was struck by its size. It appeared about 50 feet (15.2 m) tall with a wide canopy. The many pears that had matured were now rotting in the tall grass. Empty liquor bottles and fast-food take-out bags littered the area around the tree. A flattened cardboard box about five feet (1.5 m) in length laid beside the tree.

It was warm and sunny, so I sat beneath the tree because it provided shade. Listening to the vehicles whiz by above me, I remembered Arlene's ancestors and what it might have been like when life was much slower, without fast-food restaurants. I imagined sheep and goats grazing in the field; children frolicking in the haystack; ma in her long dress and white apron making fall pear butter in the kitchen; and pa whittling wood on the porch shaded by this tree. I could have continued the reverie for much longer, but didn't because of the vehicular roar above, and the observation that westward along the ditch stood a homeless camp sheltered by a small grove of trees.

Perhaps I was not alone even now. Perhaps others appreciated the Hager pear tree like me, but unlike me, depended on its bounty. These local residents were now beneficiaries of the tree. A symbol of American perseverance was sustaining Americans who had dropped out of the American way of modern life. I picked up a fallen pear to save its seeds and perpetuate its heritage somewhere else.

By 2004, the Oregon Travel Information Council had listed 32 heritage trees in their brochure, "Guide to Oregon Historical Markers and Heritage Trees." To achieve heritage status, a tree may be noteworthy in size or age for its species, but it must be associated with events or people contributing to state history. None of the heritage trees were protected by law, and all of them stood by good will alone.

In August of that year I witnessed the dedication of the state's 31st heritage tree—a bigleaf maple called the Pow Wow Tree near the Clackamas River, southeast of Portland. Maynard had told me he could not attend but hoped I would enjoy it.

I entered the City of Gladstone from Highway 99E that carried me over the Clackamas River. Clackamas Boulevard was closed to traffic for the ceremony, so I parked on a side street. I walked down Clackamas Blvd

Pow Wow tree

to find lawn chairs being set in a semicircle before an aging maple tree beside the road. Among the locals milling about someone said: "When I was a kid I used to climb in the tree. It doesn't look any different than it did 50 years ago." But it must have. Erected behind the tree stood a telephone poll from which issued cables supporting trunks growing from a large amorphous base—technically a bole. This was a grandfather maple that must have sprouted many limbs over its lifetime.

The tree stood at the edge of a front yard belonging to a one-level house. Beneath one of the tree's large, emaciated branches facing the street sat a boulder inset with two plaques. At the foot of the small boulder were stepping stones set within a neatly tended patch of gravel. For this special day and posterity stood another plaque beside the boulder, covered by a white scarf with an Indian design.

The crowd slowly grew larger as we waited for the master of ceremony to arrive. A few senior ladies posed beneath an emaciated branch for photographs. Mel, a native from the Confederated Tribes of the Grand Ronde, who was a cultural resource technician with Chinook and Calapooya lineage, stepped up to the tree and sprinkled tobacco around it. He said that spreading tobacco is a sign of respect and gratitude for the people who have gone before.

Finally the mayor of Gladstone arrived. He wore a short-sleeved shirt bearing an image of the Pow Wow tree—the city's logo—which looked more robust than the tree. "I've had a relationship with this tree for 50 years," said Wade Byers, commencing the ceremony. Wade had been the city's mayor for the past 25 years, lived in Gladstone most all his life, now lived across the street from the Pow Wow tree, and climbed it as a boy. "We knew it was a special tree then," he continued. "It was an important tree to the Native Americans and to the pioneers who moved here from the Midwest. It was the site of pow wows and probably a place for barbecues or whatever they did to celebrate during the Civil War era."

Jim Renner spoke next, on behalf of the Oregon Travel Information Council. He pointed out that Oregonian customs have been intertwined with the state's heritage trees. Then local historian Herbert Beals spoke. It is believed, he said, that the Clackamas Indians once lived in villages along the Clackamas River, and used the location of the Pow Wow tree for meetings. It is undisputed that the tree witnessed the first Clackamas County Fair in 1860 and the first state fair in 1861. Still standing across the street was a remodeled residence formerly known as the Pow Wow Inn in 1927. In 1937, Gladstone Camp Fire Girls sponsored a celebration called the Gladstone Pow-Wow and affixed a plaque to the boulder before the tree. By 1953, the tree showed signs of failing health, at which time a county horticulturalist prescribed pruning. In 1967 city council ordered its removal, but people so heartily objected that, within a month, council reversed its decision: the tree itself and its mini-acreage of hallowed ground belonged to the people of Gladstone. In 1976, the International Society of Arboriculture and the National Arborist Association honoured the tree with another plaque because it was a bicentennial tree. They estimated it had gained a root-hold when the Declaration of Independence was signed. "Now it's a heritage tree," concluded Herb, "in recognition of its perseverance to survive."

The mayor had more to say after Herb, the most interesting of which was that, when the subsequent owners of the former Pow Wow Inn renovated their home, they found a menu listing chicken dinners for 35 cents. The crowd giggled.

Then Mel and Connie from the Confederated Tribes stepped forward with Elaine, president of the Gladstone Historical Society. Mel and Connie gave gifts to the mayor, Elaine and Herb. When the white scarf with the Indian design was lifted, I could read the plaque. It proclaimed

City of
Gladstone
logo

the tree's heritage status. Mel spoke to the crowd: "When I see many people coming together to save a tree that is very much a part of everyone's past, I feel hopeful about everyone's future."

The ceremony ended and locals milled about once again, chatting with neighbours. A small crowd collected around the mayor. I overheard him say, "This is Gladstone and we do things different," and continued on about how Gladstone is a community that seeks consensus.

Several months after the dedication, I stopped in Gladstone while on a road trip northward. I wanted to photograph the Pow Wow tree. I knocked on the door of the homeowners who had consented to the telephone poll being installed in their front yard to support the tree. Leslie and Jack answered the door and I asked for permission to stand on their lawn. They invited me into their home. Leslie said she had moved here to live beside the tree.

As we looked out of their living room window at the tree, Jack and Leslie said they were members of the Baha'i Faith, and have held gatherings around the tree. They also witnessed others gather round the tree—teachers with their school children, neighbours socializing, church groups praying, and unknown others painting symbols on the hallowed asphalt beneath the tree.

"Any place where people have gathered with unity of purpose," said Jack, "there's some effect." "And that affects the community and the world," said Leslie.

᪥

Chapter Four
TREES OF HOPE
San Francisco, California

Arbor Day, March 12, 2005, San Francisco: Near the most dangerous, low-income housing project of Bayview Hunter's Point, I watched young African Americans break-dancing and hip-hopping in a park. From the crowd circling the dancers, the mayor of San Francisco stepped forward.

"The southeast of the city has been historically under served," said Gavin Newsom. "My plan for San Francisco this year is planting 5000 trees. Today we are planting 250 trees." Then with a rousing inflection, "You deserve it. It's long overdue!"

"One hundred fifty trees on Ingalls," yelled someone from the crowd. Another cheered, "Forty on Crocker," followed by "Thirty for Drew Elementary," another shouted.

"It's like an auction!" exclaimed the mayor.

But the locals were not making bids to buy ramshackle city streets and a school. Trees were sacrificing themselves to bestow grace on a desperate place. By 2005, the Urban Forest Council counted 99,000 street trees in San Francisco. An estimated 56 percent of the city was not treed. Affluent districts were more treed than poorer ones. While the San Francisco peninsula had not been heavily forested before European settlement, trees were seen to improve the city in numerous ways, ecologically, economically and socially. Planting trees was seen as community building.

A city park trooper approached the mayor and placed a tree-leaf lea around his neck. The mayor announced: "I'm clean and green. Let's go plant some trees!" As the crowd broke up, a man in a green T-shirt asked the people to welcome the Tristania family to Ingalls Street. As of 4 a.m., employees of the Department of Public Works had been planting Tristania confertas on residential streets of the Bayview. Then the mayor, surrounded by security, briskly walked a few blocks into the housing project, called the Double Rock. I followed with a small group.

We walked up to a small hole that had already been dug in a yard beside an apartment building. The mayor set a Tristania conferta into the hole. An apartment dweller timidly peeked out from behind broken blinds to watch.

The mayor and entourage walked on, outside the Double Rock onto streets of the Bayview. I followed for a while, but became bored with the routine of setting Tristania confertas in square holes of sidewalk. I turned back toward the Double Rock. Outside the Double Rock corner store a clerk was watching city workers plant trees. "More trees, less violence," he remarked. Crossing the street, I observed that the street-level windows of the Good Samaritan Church were barred by metal grates.

I returned to my car and drove onto Highway 101 going north into downtown San Francisco. Both Highway 101 and Highway 280 bordered the west and north of one of the poorest neighbourhoods in the city. Bordering the east side of the Bayview was the local superfund site, Hunters Point Naval Shipyard, and a power plant that generated 575 tons of airborne pollutants every year. (A superfund site is an uncontrolled or abandoned place in the US where hazardous waste is located.) Pollutants from these sites also mingled with the fumes from the local sewage treatment plant that handled 80 percent of San Francisco's solid wastes.

At the time in 2005, the Bayview was home to approximately 36,000 people. About 48 percent of the residents were African American, and 40 percent had annual incomes below $15,000. Living within an environment of 325 industrial sites, 100 brown fields (former industrial sites) and leaking underground fuel tanks, it's not surprising that residents suffered higher than the national average rates of asthma, breast cancer and diabetes. The Health and Environmental Resource Center on Third Street—Bayview's main street—provided asthma clinics for the locals. The Literacy for Environmental Justice centre gave "toxic tours" of the superfund site and power plant. All of these conditions are hidden from view by commuters driving into downtown San Francisco.

Also hidden from public view are the residents of San Francisco County jails. In 2005, the U.S. Bureau of Justice website reported these 2002 national statistics: The largest ethnic minority of jail inmates—an estimated 40 percent—was African American. The percentage of all inmates charged with a drug office rose from 9 percent in 1983 to 23 percent in 1989, and remained at 22 percent in 1996. Drug offenders accounted for the largest source of growth in the jails between 1996 and 2002—an increase of 37 percent.

A few months before Arbor Day 2005, I visited the San Bruno jail, hidden in the hills of San Bruno, south of the San Francisco Bay Area. To gain entry, I checked in with the guard at the gate. As I drove through, I passed by the old 1934 prison and its replacement under construction, being built to withstand earthquakes.

Driving past the jail houses, I beheld a rural scene. Fourteen acres stretched before me, filled with long, tilled rows. Near the fields for crops stood an old farm building, an old cattle and horse corral, and piles of mulch and horse manure. I parked beside a mobile office, got out of the car and surveyed the grounds. Behind me loomed two large greenhouses, one covered by plastic and the other walled with glass.

I entered the mobile office, expecting to meet Cathrine Sneed. Inside, the receptionist directed me to her office. Cathrine sat behind a folding table without a computer. She greeted me and continued to interact with her staff, who came and went, joking in a familiar way. While they talked, I observed Cathrine's garden jacket, baggy pants and work boots. She observed me as well while speaking to her staff. When they left, she turned to me.

The jail's former slaughterhouse was our first headquarters, she explained. It was unheated and everyone got cold in the winter. The first floor offered a stove for cooking meals, a sink and a tool shed. One toilet without a sink served as the restroom. "I fundraised to obtain this mobile office so that everyone could work inside heated rooms," she said.

She invited me to visit the old jail, which was still in use. We left the office and drove in separate cars to the jail's parking lot nearby. Entering the building, the front of which looked like a 1930's dam, we met Sheriff Michael Hennessey, who was talking with a prison manager. Cathrine told them about a car theft at the Double Rock. Some of her trainees whom she called "Earth Stewards"—young people getting green job skills—were car jacked Saturday night, she said.

Cathrine looked at me. "Do you know what a car jack is?" I nodded yes, pretending to know.

She continued with the sheriff: "The assailants dropped their gun as they stole the car, and the Earth Stewards picked it up and turned it in to the police. The police got back to me and asked, 'What am I doing to these African Americans from the Bayview who care about trees?'"

The sheriff and prison manager smiled like they knew the answer. Cathrine asked for a guard to take us to the sixth floor, which had been empty for a year. To get to the sixth floor, we left the main entrance lobby and walked down a long corridor, passing visiting rooms for prisoners and their relatives and friends. We stopped at the elevator, entered and ascended.

On the sixth floor, the guard led us to the cells. A central walkway separated two rows of cells. The cells looked about 6 feet x 12 feet (1.8 m x 3.6 m), each containing a bed, that is, a metal frame bolted to the wall, a metal toilet and a sink. The guard said the prisoners ate at long tables in the walkway between the cell rows. Prisoners were allowed no more than four pounds of books and magazines in their cells. They could go outside two times a week. Those who lived here waiting for their sentences might stay several weeks to months. When the jail was overcrowded, with some cells containing two beds and two prisoners, there was more violence.

When we returned to the elevator to descend, I realized that I was holding in my stomach, imagining the tension that must have continuously pervaded the cells. As we left the jail lobby, Cathrine joked with the guards she knew. Conversation focused on the matter of helping her Earth Stewards get driving permits. "When I first started to work at the jail in 1980, I bicycled," she said. "The prisoners taught me how to drive!"

I began to relax as we walked to the parking lot. Cathrine remarked that most of the prisoners can read and write only at the second or third grade level. "It's way cheaper to give these men and women job skills after prison," she said. "Most of them expect to go to jail again—it's just something you do."

On another visit to the San Bruno jail farm, Cathrine showed me inside the greenhouses and we walked along the fields. We had tea at her former office, the slaughterhouse. As we sat on the second floor deck and warmed ourselves in the sun, she told me more of her story.

Over 20 years ago, Cathrine worked inside the San Bruno jail, providing legal services to prisoners. In 1982 she got a deadly kidney disease. At the hospital, a friend gave her *The Grapes of Wrath* to read. She understood it to mean that if people could connect to Nature and the Earth, they could have hope and their lives would be better.

Cathrine wondered what would happen if she could bring the prisoners outside the jail: "One of my experiences in working with them was that they were so hopeless in terms of their outlook of the world. They didn't feel they had a future. They really didn't have a future. They were fighting and arguing within the jail. Seeing them leave and then come back—it was horrific just to watch. I think that's why I got sick, watching all this horrible stuff going on and also feeling it was in fact hopeless. And the prisoners looked so much like myself—young and black."

Cathrine
Sneed

From her hospital bed, Cathrine told Sheriff Hennessey that she wanted to take the prisoners outside the jail. He said OK, thinking she had a few months to live. But he thought, Holy cow! How can we do this because normally you don't take prisoners out of the jail very much. To everyone's surprise, Cathrine got better. Outdoor gardening on the jail's 14-acre (5.6-ha) farmland began.

"I couldn't walk. They would carry me out from the jail and leave me in a heap and I'd say, 'Do this and this.' They worked hard. They didn't have enough clothes on. It was cold. They had thin pants and flip-flops and they would come out and work so hard. I would think, 'What happened out here?' And the deputies would say, 'What are you doing with these people out here? They come back so nice and wonderful and helpful. And they don't get in trouble anymore.'"

Cathrine went into remission and garden work became a jail routine. Deputies guarded the prisoners as they hoed, seeded, weeded, and harvested. When jail terms came to an end—terms that averaged 30 days to 8 months with a maximum of one year, of which 60 percent of the offences were drug-related—the prisoners did not want to go home. She said most of them didn't have a home.

Home ground for many of the prisoners was Bayview Hunter's Point. Catherine advised me not to pay a visit there, but I did anyway—several times.

It was shortly after 3 p.m. during a weekday when I walked down Third Street—Bayview's main street. On the wall of a corner store were scrawled the handwritten words, "No loitering on these premesses." As I paused to note the misspelling, a red car sped up to the corner and stopped. A few of the loitering youth swaggered up to the passenger door. I watched something pass between hands, and then the red car sped down the street. I turned to walk in the other direction, pretending not to notice. I beheld the street trees. Most were dusty because Third Street was being excavated, preparing for a light rail system to connect the Bayview to downtown San Francisco. A woman wearing a frilly, ankle-length skirt of many colours and a drab brown jacket walked up and down the street, back and forth, passing me several times. She saw me looking at the street trees, in particular the one without branches standing in its sidewalk hole near a sagging, wooden shanty. When I walked back to my car I passed a man wearing a plastic wrap over his hair, standing outside a hair salon and smoking a cigarette. I remarked about the barren tree. He said that he had watched a man on cocaine destroy a tree on the street. "No respect," he said, shaking his curlers.

The next time I went to the Bayview, I picked up Anthony Travis. I drove to a parking lot of the only supermarket in town. Entering the lot I noticed a Krispy Kreme banner on the storefront, luring customers inside for donuts. I recalled Cathrine telling me that residents of the Bayview had limited access to fresh produce. I parked and Anthony led me over to a metal railing that bordered one side of the parking lot. Below us stretched a long narrow garden beside a long white warehouse. On the wall of the warehouse were painted scenes of sunflowers and happy people with bags of vegetables. Today the garden grew only shrubs, weeds and grass. Green tarps covered raised beds. At the far end of the lot stood the Bayview police station.

I looked down again at the narrow lot, scrutinizing the raised beds for pioneer veggie sprouts. Anthony looked down with me and leaned over the railing, his dreadlocks brushing his shoulders. It was a Monday morning, he recalled, when he and his cousin showed up at this former garden.

"Cathrine came up to us, sayin', 'You all here to work?' We told her yes. She said, 'I don't want to hear anythin' else. Go back there and make some beds.' I'll never forget it. I thought there was some mattress back there an' we were gonna pull some sheets back."

Anthony had been released from prison for the second time. He was 27 years old with children to care for and no job skills. "I had to do somethin' with myself. If you're not gonna hire an ex-con to do anythin', then they're just gonna go back to doin' what they used to do."

Tree on Third
Street, Bayview
Hunters Point

While in jail, Anthony had participated in Cathrine's Horticulture Program. He looked forward to "goin' to horticulture" because he could get outside the jail to get peace of mind. "It was a terrible experience as far as bein' locked up, as far as not bein' able to go anywhere," he said. "We sit in a cage jus' about all day. I was seein' fights, I was seein' people gettin' their heads bust open. It was jus' a terrible experience."

When Anthony got out of jail the first time, he had looked for jobs. "There was no job to be found. I'm a black man, I been arrested for drugs. I'm the baddest person on the planet Earth. That's the way people look at us, but it's really not so. I was tryin' to provide for my family. I was tryin' to have the nice things that I see Michael Jordan have. I wanted them things, an' that's the way a lot a kids think. They want them things. I felt that no one would hire me an' I got kids. At that time I had three kids to support. I wasn't gonna let them starve. . . . So I ended up goin' back to the dope." Anthony got arrested again for drug dealing and went to prison for three more years.

In the meantime, Cathrine had leased the Bayview lot in between the supermarket and warehouse. She called it the Garden Project. When Anthony got out of jail again, Cathrine offered him a job. She taught him how to make beds, plant seeds and water.

Anthony continued to recall: "She told me this is how you start learnin', how you start lookin' forward to different things that become a challenge in your life." At first he said he didn't understand.

Anthony and Cathrine took vegetables from the Bayview garden into the low-income housing projects where Anthony grew up. "We would set a table out and take all the vegetables and put it on the table and tell everybody livin' in the projects, if you want to have some vegetables, come out here. You should a seen how many different families was comin' out, grabbin' fruits an' vegetables an' oranges an' apples. Some kids never had certain types of fruits that we had up there. Their mom and daddy never bought it cuz they couldn't afford it. Me and Cathrine did that. We was goin' to all the different projects, different areas. Cathrine Sneed, that lady is a beautiful person. To make sure those kids eat, she don't care if your mommy on crack or your daddy on crack, or whatever the case it was, she made sure a lot of them kids ate fruits and vegetables."

To pay the Garden Project employees, Cathrine grew trees at the jail and sold them to the San Francisco Department of Public Works (DPW). Tree planting at the jail led to a DPW contract in 1992 to employ ex-offenders to plant trees on city streets.

Garden Project site

Anthony kept talking: "So then she said, Anthony, you doin' such a good job, I'm gonna let you go into the Tree Corps. The Tree Corps was another part of the Garden Project. The Tree Corps was when you graduate from the garden," he said. "You ride on the city trucks and you plant trees throughout the city for the city."

The job was hard labour. "I had to dig holes up to my neck," Anthony continued. "We planted palm trees on Mission Street about five-six years ago and we had to actually dig the holes ourselves. We had a crane to load the palm tree down in the dirt in the hole. Then we had to shovel the dirt back in there—a lot of dirt! We dug so much dirt we were actually jumpin' down in the hole throwin' the dirt out."

Anthony carried gallons of water and dirt on his back and cracked the sidewalk concrete. In the Bayview, he said people came out of their houses and begged him to plant trees. "I can't do it like this, I told 'em. But they were like, 'I'll bust the concrete myself!'

"I was just learnin' all about trees," he said. "An' then I see myself watchin' trees that I planted grow. And Cathrine walked up to me sometime. She said, 'Now Anthony, this is part of you. This is somethin' you can go and tell your kids 10 or 15 years later that you did for the city. You can go and point out a tree and say, I planted that tree. Your kids prob'ly won't believe you, but you know deep down inside that you really planted that tree. Sometime I take my kids an' we ride down the street an' I say, 'You know, I planted that tree an' that tree.' Sometime my wife say, 'I don't even want to hear about it no more!'"

I had lost track of time, leaning against the railing and listening to Anthony. I noticed a young man in disheveled clothes enter the parking lot. He walked to the entrance of the market and stopped, looking agitated. Anthony advised returning to the car.

In the 1990s, Sheriff Hennessey commissioned a study to evaluate the success of Cathrine's job training programs. The study followed 300 ex-offenders over three years. Within less than half a year of their release, 29 percent of the general release population had been arrested again, compared to only 6 percent of the Bayview Garden Project workers. After two years of release, 55 percent of the general population were arrested, while only 24 percent of former Garden Project workers returned to jail. In 1999, the cost to incarcerate one prisoner at the San Francisco County Jail was $73.78 a day, or $26,929 a year.

In 2000, Cathrine dismantled the Bayview garden. Although compost had created the soil, she feared that local contaminants were poisoning the produce. In August of that year, a fire started in Hunters Point Shipyard. During World War II, ships subjected to atomic weapon tests were decontaminated there, and radioactive waste was packaged for disposal at sea. The August 2000 fire burned 14 acres (5.6 ha) of shipyard landfill containing liquid chemical waste, asbestos, dredge spoil materials, sandblast grit solvent wastes, low-level radioactive wastes, and unknown wastes from a commercial ship repair company whose lease of the land was cancelled in 1986 for improper waste disposal. Five acres (2 ha) of the 2000 fire smoldered for at least one month directly below a hill of low-income housing, a Boys and Girls Club and a recreation centre.

When Cathrine left the Bayview garden behind, she was diagnosed with a potentially fatal thyroid disease. She recovered. She renamed the jail's horticulture program the Garden Project and employed ex-offenders to work alongside prisoners at the jail farm, which she rented for $1 a year. The produce was donated to San Francisco food banks and soup kitchens.

When the Tree Corps reached an annual budget of $500,000, it employed a crew of 12 or more to plant and water trees, most of which took root in poor neighbourhoods with few trees. Anthony became a Tree Corps supervisor. He estimates that he planted about 5000 trees— half of the trees planted by the Tree Corps. He learned how to plant trees with root restrictors to keep the roots anchored in the ground, how to prune trees, and how to care for the different kinds.

In 2001, Anthony became a model of Tree Corps success. He graduated from the Tree Corps to work directly for DPW, cleaning city streets. He worked hard to support his family, which by then was a wife and six kids. After three and a half years of work at DPW, he hoped for a permanent position and benefits. But budget cuts loomed and Anthony worried.

A few weeks before DPW laid off Anthony, the Tree Corps cared for its last tree. Cathrine worried about the effect of budget cuts on her programs and staff. About 4500 ex-offenders and youth-at-risk had worked in the horticulture program, the Garden Project, and the Tree Corps. At the same time, they got help with getting drivers licenses, GED certificates, working through family problems, and paying child support.

Then a new door opened. The Public Utilities Commission (PUC) teamed with Cathrine to provide job training for at-risk individuals, young adults and high school students, many of whom came from the Bayview. She called them Earth Stewards. They would take college classes, work at the jailhouse farm, and maintain PUC land—900 acres (364.2 ha) surrounding the city's reservoirs, pump stations and right-of-ways. Some of the land required cleanup of debris left in the woods by the homeless. Anthony was hired to supervise.

Tree Corps
at work in
San Francisco

Cathrine invited me on a clean-up. The day began about 7 a.m. with breakfast served at the jailhouse farm. The Earth Stewards were given steel-toed boots to wear. The boots were donated because they could not afford them.

We drove to the back woods of Laguna Honda, in the centre of San Francisco. Some of the Earth Stewards donned masks to protect against pollutants because, coming from the Bayview, they had asthma. Tools in hand, we descended onto an unofficial trail into the woods. Shelters roofed by branches populated the ravine floor, also littered with other human remains.

When we stopped, Cathrine took a rake from among the tools that were carried. She bent over some debris and looked up at the crew gathered around her. "This is how to rake," she said, and raked with full force to pile debris on the ground. She looked up as she demonstrated, making sure she had everyone's eyes. By the way everyone watched her, I wondered if the Earth Stewards had ever raked before.

During a break, Anthony told me he learned how to supervise by watching Catherine, who showed how to work by working. For this crew, he was also a peer counsellor: "I'm on 'em 101. I say look, you can make a choice. You can end up dead in a casket, you can end up locked up, your kids come to see you in the look glass. You can end up out there saggin' on the corner, on drugs, hopped out, on crack or whatever. But you can end up doin' the right thing, takin' care of your family. An' I talk to a lot of them. I set them and told them part of my life. I done these things that you think ain't nobody in the world done. You think you being slick. This one guy, he's working with us right now, he's just a jack of all trades, he a jack—pow pow. I always set down and talk to this guy every day. I tell him, there was a guy that used to work with us, he was the same way you are, and he dead now."

In April 2005, 12 Earth Stewards graduated to join the PUC apprenticeship program, which would pay them to become state-certified journeymen and women, able to work anywhere in the construction industry. Upon graduation, they would be eligible to apply for permanent city jobs, like what Anthony had hoped for.

I picked up Anthony for another tour of the Bayview. As I drove, he talked about the financial difficulties of his lay-off. A permanent job with DPW would have allowed him to buy a home and rise up from his roots. We drove through the projects where Anthony's parents had lived when they moved to the Bayview when he was 14. Anthony pointed out all the trees he planted on LaSalle, Innes, Engels, Cargo, Evans, Hudson, Cashmere, Keith, Cesar Chavez, Royelle, and Third. He said, "Third Street was one of our main areas that we kept watering, making sure that it was watered heavily."

As we drove near Third Street I found a place to park. We walked up and down the street and discovered that most of the trees he planted there were now gone. We suspected that the city's light rail project had called for removal of trees that were failing or would be damaged by construction. Those trees would be replaced by the Tristania conferta because of the species' ability to withstand vandalism, soil toxicity and water deprivation. Another difference between the Tristania conferta— the species planned for Third Street, and the Tristania laurina—the species planted by the Tree Corps, is that the conferta grows faster.

"You can put a light rail through," said Anthony, "you can put trees through here, but the people, if it's still the same type of people still livin' the same way, still havin' the same problems, it's gonna be the same environment." Or worse. I had read in a Bayview newspaper that some residents feared that improvements would lead to gentrification and rental hikes they could not afford.

Walking down the street on Third near Van Dyke amid hard hats, big trucks, engine noise, and barriers blocking the sidewalk, Anthony and I found one Tristania laurina that he had planted. It seemed to me to be a more suitable species for the Bayview. The laurina is more tolerant and more elegant. It produces small yellow flowers among clusters of slender leaves, and promises a fuller canopy to shade pedestrians.

I asked Anthony if I could photograph him standing beneath his tree. As he looked up into the canopy, withered from construction dust but still green, I photographed hope. Cathrine had planted hope.

SHARON McCANN

§♥

Chapter Five
TREE ORIENTED
Seattle, Washington

I was having coffee with Cass Turnbull in her home in Seattle. She was telling me about a self-actualization seminar she took in the 1980s and what she decided to do. While pruning wasn't the most important thing in life, she said bad pruning annoyed her. And tree topping as a form of bad pruning really annoyed her. Cass was a certified landscaper and arborist. I had noticed the very nicely pruned Japanese maple that graced the front door of her home as I entered it.

"When I told people I was going to end tree-topping," she said, "it was like, 'Here's this loony toon gal!' I sort of compare it to the first mad mother who said she was going to end drunk driving. When the first person said this has got to end, the problem was so prevalent, so pervasive, it was like, 'You can't do that.' There's still drunk driving but nobody doubts that changes have been made."

Cass founded PlantAmnesty in 1987. At the time, topping trees for views was popular, given that hills and ridges abound in Seattle. Seattle real estate views are even classified—territorial views, peek-a-boo views, directional views, mountain views, and water views. When PlantAmnesty got into gear, it offered: pruning classes; free pruning for those who can't pay for it; a newsletter; photo contests of malpruned shrubs or ugly topiary; a how-to-prune video; two TV public service announcements; pruning literature, including a brochure titled "6 Ways to Kill Your Tree"; and anti-topping protests led by Cass.

"Has it made a difference?" I asked.

Seattle tree
topiary

She said PlantAmnesty had grown to 800 members by 2005. And over the last 15 years, the number of tree-topping ads had decreased from 63 percent to 8 percent.

"When I started out, trees were below shrubs in importance to the general public," said Cass. "It was like a joke. So you're like a tree saviour? Ha, ha. And then there was a revolution of tree consciousness. I still have some of the magazines. One year a tree showed up on the cover of *Time* magazine, right after global warming hit the news. The status of trees has risen many notches from when I first started Plant Amnesty."

In 1996 PlantAmnesty launched Seattle's heritage tree program in partnership with the city. Within nine years of its existence, by 2005, 26 heritage trees graced the City of Seattle. City residents were proud of their heritage trees and keen for more of them. By the summer of that year, they had nominated a record number of trees for heritage status. Twelve were selected for consideration and Cass invited me to tag along with the evaluators.

We collected at Cass' house to get our assignments. Everyone, except me, was either an arborist with at least 10 years' experience or a sophisticated tree lover. Unsophisticated tree lovers, according to Cass, would lobby for a tree they loved, or lobby for a tree because the tree owner was important to them. Heritage tree evaluators had to be tree-oriented.

The evaluators divided into two groups. We would traverse a city of 91.5 square miles (236.9 sq km) within a few hours. Cass insisted that Arthur Lee Jacobson travel in her car. Arthur knew a lot about trees. He knew: a tree's common name, scientific name, its subspecies or varieties; how many cultivars it has; whether it's a mixed hybrid—half-southern or half-East Asian, for example; where it comes from and where it is grows in Seattle; and of those, if there are several, which is the most or least robust. I had met Arthur before, and attended a city park tour that he led. When he spoke about hybrids and cultivars, people asked him if he was a botanist or something. He replied that he was a plant expert. He was also a plant historian. He could remember when a certain bay tree was no bigger than a bush until they stopped pruning it. He also knew that there was only one bay tree at Green Lake Park.

Liz Ellis invited me to travel in her van. Liz was an arborist who worked for the Department of Transportation. She volunteered for the Heritage Tree program because there was no city budget for it. Others riding in her van were Mark, Ron and Tina—all arborists. En route, Mark marvelled that Arthur didn't drive a car to work. "If you take a chainsaw on the city bus," he said, "you have to look very non-threatening." He asked me if I had a copy of Arthur's book, *Trees of Seattle*, for reference, but I didn't.

We drove to the home of an ungainly beech that shaded the front yard of a residence. Liz parked and the team jumped out of the van, holding checklists on clipboards. We approached the tree and just looked at it. Some thought it was notable. Liz said it was not highly notable: "Would I go out of my way to visit this tree?" I sensed the answer was no. A notable tree has the potential to be a heritage tree, said Tina. I assumed that a notable tree was a heritage tree in training. I was beginning to think like the tree-oriented.

Leaving behind the beech, we travelled to the location of a mountain ash. As soon as we entered the backyard and approached the tree, the evaluators went to work. While Tina looked at wounds on the split trunks, Ron pounded the trunk with a mallet to look for rot. Everyone else checked off their forms, rating the tree for its health, location value and risk of failure. They all agreed the tree was the biggest mountain ash in the city and a fine one for its species. Then the homeowner entered the yard. She looked at the tree and then at us, downcast. She said her husband liked the tree but she did not. Liz replied that they would recommend it for heritage status, but the homeowners would have to agree to accept it. If they did, they could place a plaque or stone beneath the tree, but they would have to pay for it. Even then, the tree would not be protected. Even so, Tina said heritage tree recognition shows that tree love is going on. I guessed that Tina was a sophisticated tree-lover.

I had another opportunity to evaluate more trees that summer. Arthur accepted my offer to drive him around Seattle to examine trees for the overdue second edition of his book, *Trees of Seattle*. Without a vehicle, he travelled by carpooling, riding the city bus, or cycling. He had decided in high school not to drive for the health of the planet. Riding in cars restricted his senses, he told me. He preferred to interact with trees by touching them, smelling them, and eating their leaves and flowers. As a plant expert for hire, he usually worked without gloves.

The project to update his book required that Arthur revisit every tree listed in the first edition. He would also check out new trees that came to his attention. He knew it was worth the effort. The first edition published in 1989 was so popular that I could not find one copy at the Seattle Public Library. By 2005 you could pay more than $99.99 on Amazon.com for a new copy of the first edition, or $58 for a used one. The city arborist had told me that the book made his job easier: "When new homeowners move in and want to cut down a big tree because they don't want to rake leaves, I could show them the book and say, 'This tree has been documented as notable. Have fun raking leaves for the next 20 years.' Usually they reconsidered."

Arthur told me that he had been contacted about a tulip tree. The homeowners hoped it would be declared the biggest in Seattle in Arthur's second edition. So we drove to West Seattle to check out the tree. While I stood on the sidewalk, Arthur knocked on the front door of the house to ask permission to measure the tree. Arthur always asked for permission when trees stood on private property, even if the trees stood beside the sidewalk. He told me that he had returned as many as five times to find someone home.

The homeowner opened the door and talked with Arthur on his front porch. I could hear the owner say, "It was topped in 1983. I can't believe it was topped." Arthur smiled and said, "Lots of trees got topped." We just stood for a while to appreciate the tree's expansive canopy. The owner remarked that it took several truckloads to remove tulip tree leaves in the fall.

Arthur left the porch to wrap a tape measure around the trunk. He declared the circumference to be 14 feet 5.5 inches (4.4 m). He stepped back into the street with a laser rangefinder to measure the height. "Eighty-five feet (25.9 m) tall does not make it the biggest tulip tree in Seattle," he said, scribbling measurements in the margin of his first edition. "The biggest one is 120 feet (36.6 m) tall, with a 15-foot 9.5-inch (4.8 m) circumference, near the Seattle Tennis Club." The owner laughed: "Maybe we should give it Miracle-Gro®!" Arthur replied, "If you want it to get bigger, water it." He delivered important words like boxcars on a train, staccato-like and weighty, articulating the letter "T."

Arthur Lee
Jacobson

We gawked again at the tulip tree's canopy. Arthur told the owner he would note in his second edition that it is a beautiful tree even though it was topped. As we drove away, Arthur explained that topping does not necessarily shorten a tree's life, and that trees are topped by the wind, but it was malpruning to top a tree. He said that properly pruning a big old tree like the tulip could easily cost $1000, which showed that the owners valued the tree more than money. Another sign of being tree-oriented, I noted.

Next we drove to the east side of West Seattle to measure a black walnut tree. It was the fourth Seattle heritage tree to be recognized. Arthur wanted to measure it to see if it deserved mention in his second edition. It had not been included in the first edition because other black walnuts were bigger and more visible to the public. He said he followed his own principles for including trees in his book to dissuade public claims of favouritism. The principles were: "Big rather than small, old rather than young, healthy rather than sickly, attractive rather than ugly, and on public rather than on private land." Arthur followed his own principles of attire too: cargo pants, white shirt, and salt and pepper wavy hair, shoulder-length.

I parked beside a pink, well preserved home on a hilltop with a view. Arthur went to knock on the door, leaving me to stand on the sidewalk again. A lean, sprightly lady in her 80s answered the door and emerged, smiling. She escorted us into her yard, which sat adjacent to her home and the sidewalk. When she and Arthur stopped to talk about her tree, I scanned the garden, finding birdhouses, shells, stones, driftwood sculptures, and ceramic frogs and cupids. A weeping birch that had been topped for a water view framed a corner of the yard. A small laurel tree stood in the middle of the yard. It's canopy had been pruned like a mushroom, and contained wind chimes and a stuffed owl. Behind the laurel, at the back of the yard, a large black walnut interrupted the fence by its trunk. On the fence near the tree hung a long mirror. At the base of the tree stood a sign. I walked to the sign and read it:

Heritage Tree, Black Walnut . . . . This individual combines impressive size, respectable age, and handsome appearance. Its tremendous width of branching stands out prominently. Hence it not only lends cooling shade, but its noble presence makes it a local landmark. PlantAmnesty Heritage Tree Project 98.1

Arthur took out his tape measure from his backpack and returned to the sidewalk to measure the width of the canopy. The proud tree owner looked on, smiling. Arthur announced the tree was 69 feet (21 m) tall and 9 feet 7.25 inches (2.9 m) around, with a canopy that averaged about 78 feet (23.8 m). Arthur thanked the woman and we departed. In the car he told me her name was Vivian McLean.

On our way to check out more trees, Arthur looked up page 339 of his book. "A black walnut in Volunteer Park is taller and has a thicker trunk," he said. "If a tree is in a park, I am more apt to list that one. Vivian's tree is beautiful but not very accessible to visitors, so I doubt it will get squished into the book." The second edition would include perhaps 400 more trees, he said, bringing the total trees to over 1000 without a significant increase in pages. Vivian is a great lady, an activist in her community, he added, but that does not add merit to the tree. Arthur said he was tree-oriented.

Vivian's black walnut tree

About six months later, in 2006, Arthur published the second edition of *Trees of Seattle*. He mailed me a copy. I looked up black walnuts in the book and discovered that Vivian's heritage tree was not listed. Another black walnut heritage tree was listed, however. It was shorter than Vivian's, but its trunk was stouter and canopy wider, and it stood in a corner of the yard beside a sidewalk, making it more accessible to public view. I knew that Arthur's principles had ruled. But there was something else about Vivian's tree that, I believed, deserved honourable mention in a book about Seattle trees. Vivian had given her black walnut tree the legal right to live for the duration of its lifespan. No one in Seattle had ever done that before.

Cass had informed me that when Vivian's black walnut became a heritage tree, she suggested Vivian protect it in perpetuity through a conservation easement. Vivian consented, and on October 15, 1998, the papers were registered with King County. Plant Amnesty was charged with ensuring that the tree was properly maintained by Vivian and successive property owners, unless an act of God made its life a hazard, at which point it could be removed, respectfully. If anyone were to damage, remove or top the tree to increase property value, the assessed increase in value would be included in the fine.

Vivian seemed tree-oriented to me. There must be something more about the tree, beyond its size and stature, that motivated Vivian to give it civil rights.

In the summer of 2006, I went to visit Vivian. When I arrived, I knocked on the front door of her pink house, and she emerged, smiling as usual. She invited me to sit with her in the garden and led me to a small table with chairs on the lawn. When she went to make ice tea, I admired the black walnut. Its wide canopy reached outward over the lawn and shaded me. Feather-like leaves cascaded from arching branches, wafting in the light wind and sounding like distant ocean waves.

When Vivian returned, she brought two tall glasses of ice tea on a tray and sat down beside me. I remarked that I had noticed her tree did not get mention in Arthur's second edition. I said Arthur had told me that lack of public access was a factor. Vivian just smiled. She said that she often invited pedestrians into her yard by way of posted garden signs near the sidewalk. Sometimes she would call out to people walking by and invite them into the yard. We looked at her tree. She said a few neighbours had wanted her to cut down the tree because it's not a clean tree. When the walnuts drop, she said, their green outer skins rot on the ground. The nut does not mature in Seattle; it just turns into a little rock. When the leaves fall, the centres of the leaves stick into the ground. It's a difficult tree to live with, she agreed, but easier to live with than some people. Vivian said she became an activist in the 1960s, "when activism was a dirty word":

"There's 13 districts in the city," she continued, "and we had to fight to become one. They wanted us to be with West Seattle. I refused and everybody else here did too because over there they have condos. Over here we have apartments. Over there, they're all white. Over here we're just a variety of colours. They didn't want us shopping over there, even though our money is as good as anybody else's. They didn't want minorities to come into the west side and they fought it forever. So we decided we had to have a district ourselves, and that's what we did."

She explained that the City of Seattle divided itself into 13 neighbourhood districts in 1987. The goal was to promote participation in the community. West Seattle was divided into two districts—Delridge and Southwest. Delridge was so named because it's located in a valley between two ridges. Vivian and her husband had purchased their Delridge home in 1948, and later purchased the adjacent lot with the black walnut. They raised four children there. Their house sat on one of the few view tops of Delridge.

"All the 13 districts of Seattle come together now and tell what they're doing to learn from each other. And that's what we need to do, is learn from each other. When I started doing it, to get them off the front porch was quite a job, and to look beyond their own land. They're all working people and they don't have much time. For them to see the neighbourhood was another step, and then to see the neighbourhood next to it. Some have seen the whole city."

Vivian said that in 2002, the district named a new building on Delridge Avenue after her, but the most important thing was that the building helped the people. It contained rent-subsidized apartments, the first library in Delridge, the Delridge Neighborhoods Development Association, and a cafe.

Vivian's steel blue eyes looked into mine. Now and then she would admire her garden. Now and then I would look at the mirror on the fence beside the black walnut. The mirror held the image of the garden, suggesting it was a place for reflection. I began to feel calmer in this refuge.

I said that I had discovered in Arthur's book that the black walnut was used to fight in World War I. I pulled out the book from my bag and read this passage:

Prior to World War I, German agents tried to buy supplies in Pennsylvania, for few woods (or none) are so ideal for gunstocks and aeroplane propellers. While the war was being fought, a slogan was 'Fight with your walnut trees!'

Vivian
McLean

Vivian agreed about the power of the walnut. She said she had even written a poem about it. She got up to search for it in her house and returned. During her battles for Delridge, she said, she would go out late at night and stand beneath her black walnut tree. She said it was her "Night-time Cure" and read this out loud:

Sometimes I cannot sleep at night,
Especially when the moon is bright.
I walk outside to view the sight
Through tree branches late at night.
It eases out the awful fright
Of things I know that just aren't right
I'm not at all good in a fight.
I get upset and get real tight. . . .

Vivian put down her poem and looked at her tree for a while. Then she looked at me and said, "On this lot you can build several houses. To a developer that means money, and the person who owns the land will get a better price for selling his house. Most of the young under 50 or 60 years really don't know the value of trees. They love them. They like to see them out in the woods. They like them in their yard until it cuts down on what they're going to make profit out of. I think we've changed our world. Our houses are so close together that we don't look for trees to sit under, because next door there's a house 10 feet (3.05 m) away, and that house is 10 feet away from the next house. The backyards are small. If parents grow a tree, it takes 10, 15 years from the time a kid is born to the time he's playing soccer, and then he doesn't want to sit in the backyard."

I thought about the places I had lived as a child in California. I couldn't remember any trees and rarely lived in houses with backyards. Mostly we lived in apartments. A few shrubs surfaced in my memories.

We continued to drink ice tea and enjoy the shade of the black walnut. Vivian remembered sitting in her backyard as a child in Michigan. When summers got hot, she said, she liked the shade of their black walnut tree. She liked shucking walnuts, even though the husks stained her hands.

Vivian said she was born after World War I and grew up on a farm. They raised radishes, raspberries and alfalfa, and everyone worked on the farm. It was the kids' job to collect the black walnuts. She said: "You had a board that had a knot hole in it, and it had to be the right size. You would hack the walnut when it still had the shuck on, the outside green thing. And then inside was the brown nut. Getting the shuck off was fun. You put it over the knothole, and the nut fell through the board into a pail below. And then you'd take all those nuts, when you had time, and put them on a flat rock and used a hammer to break the nut. And then you picked it out. We'd save them for the wintertime and eat them like you would any other nuts instead of potato chips. We didn't have those kinds of things. We just had plain black walnuts for a treat. But we used them a lot in cookies and cakes and things like that."

She also liked to swing on the tree and play in it. "Yes the walnut tree was a fun place," she said, smiling again. "It was a good friend."

In the very next moment, I felt sad that I never had a tree for a friend, and wanted one now.

❧

Chapter Six
FOREST DEFENDERS
Willamette National Forest, Oregon

Perusing an issue of the *Eugene Weekly*, I noticed a short item in the newspaper titled "Record Treesit": April 20, 2001 marked the three-year anniversary of what was claimed to be the longest and highest treesit in North America. By this time, activists had occupied trees in the Willamette National Forest for 1100 days to protect 94 acres (38 ha) of old-growth. When the US Forest Service sold the trees for logging in 1998, an environmental coalition appealed to the court for not surveying for species at risk. The fragmented patches of forest had never been logged, and contained cathedral-like trees in a low-elevation, Douglas-fir and western hemlock forest. Some of the trees were estimated to be 400 years old.

Treesitting had become more common, I noticed, but as an occupation, it did not come with benefits or even a wage. Given that, I wondered what motivated the activists, who were most likely twenty-somethings without a regular job or a mortgage.

Driving through Eugene, Oregon, I located the office of Cascadia Forest Defenders in an old brick building on Willamette St. next door to the Morning Glory Cafe. Inside the brick building were several offices of other environmental groups, including one promoting red worms. I knocked on the door of the forest defenders but nobody answered. So I just read the posters on a bulletin board outside their office.

Among the posters about treesitting villages in Oregon was one with a map to Fall Creek. It was this village that currently enjoyed fame for its duration. Drawings of triumphant treesitters crossing roped bridges between tall trees illustrated the map. The poster said "Interested in defending ancient forests? . . . It's easy!" I doubted it was easy, but directions to the village were clear. By way of hand-drawn maps, directions pointed south of Eugene, through the town of Lowell, past Dolly Varden Campground and into the Willamette National Forest.

During the summer of 2001 in the mid-morning I ascended the potholed Forest Service Road #1817 into the national forest. On the way up the mountainside, I passed teenaged locals who were packing a carton of empty beer bottles in the trunk of their car. Their nonchalance seemed a bit odd to me, given the entrenched rebellion that I expected to lie ahead.

I drove a few more miles and parked before a road-wide banner that proclaimed "Red Cloud Thunder—The forest we defend will forever stand! No more stumps. No deal, assholes." Behind the banner, buckets and signs hung from ropes tied to nearby trees. The blockade stretched before me about 100 feet (30.5 m). I read a sign hanging with vertebrae and thigh bones that said: "Blessed are those who come with love and good intentions. Welcome friends." Another sign said: "Warned are those who come with hate and destruction. Leave or bad omens will befall you."

Banner before entrance to Fall Creek Treesit

Despite my good intentions, I walked warily beneath the buckets, clutching a plastic bag containing a donation of food. Proceeding forward I could see another barricade up ahead. Getting closer, I beheld a teepee without walls supporting a platform topped by a blue tarp. As I approached, a sentry sprang up from the platform. His face was framed by gray and tangled dreadlocks. He did not smile.

"Hi, I've come to visit," I said, extending my quivering arm that held the bag. "I've brought some food." No response. "Thanks for defending the forest," I said. A broad, partly toothless grin broke out and I quickly walked around the barricade.

Barricade close-up

Behind the barricade stood another blue-tarped roof structure. It appeared to be a supply centre. I set down my bag of oatmeal and rice beside big boxes of tired vegetables. A few feet away laid sleeping bodies in tattered sleeping bags, smelling of alcohol.

I looked around. The supply centre occupied part of the dirt logging road that continued into the forest. On a side of the road walking in the forest was a young man with shaggy hair. As he approached, I recognized him as a treesitter I had met earlier. He had warned me that treesitters at Fall Creek had driven out a journalist who wanted to write about sex in the trees.

"Hi Tangent!" I called out. Tangent smiled with recognition and walked up to me on the road. We hugged like old friends. Tangent had recently changed his name from Shaggy, which suited his hairstyle. Tangent had also told me that it was common practice among treesitters to change names to protect their identities.

"Would you like me to show you around Fall Creek?" he asked. "It's about time to deliver food to the treesitters."

"Sure," I said, relieved. I was feeling uncomfortable as the hung-over villagers began to rise from their bedding and walk about. Defences must have been slack during the night, I assumed. But treesitters could relax a bit, now that the Forest Service road closure, imposed for nearly two years, had been recently ruled unlawful. I glanced at another banner hanging behind the barricade. It read: "Don't squash free speech."

Tangent picked up several boxes of vegetables and balanced them on his shoulder. With the muscle and demeanour of a friendly bear, he led me into the forest along a well-worn, narrow path. Up ahead stood a cluster of five tall trees. As we approached, I could see ropes connecting the upper canopies of four of the trees. Two trees supported a platform roped between them, about 150 feet (45.7 m) above ground.

I knew a few things about this cluster of trees, having researched treesitter websites beforehand. In front of us, from right to left, stood Granma, Yggdrasill, Kali Ma, Happy and Fang'orn. Fang'orn was claimed to be the highest tree occupied at Fall Creek and the highest treesit (207 feet, 63.1 m) in the world. Treesitters reported that they had invited the *Guinness Book of World Records* to confirm their claim, but staff had declined to visit.

Walking toward the base of the trees, we followed a path lined by small rocks. The designated path appeared to protect tree roots. Two women and a young man emerged from sleeping bags on the ground. Tangent and I sat down on a log beside them. The women flashed straight white teeth as they complained to Tangent about revelries the night before. They complained about the mother who visited with her baby and fed it beer. Forest defence is no place for a baby, they said.

After small talk, we left to deliver food to another treesit. "Not everyone is right for treesitting," said Tangent. "We asked a treesitter to leave after he came down to get toilet paper in town." He admitted that he himself had decided to stay on the ground after falling 50 feet (15 m) on a line.

I knew that accidents happened to others too, such as losing hair in a rappel, getting frostbite on toes, or worse. One treesitter had woken up at night to pee, and while heading for the "bathroom," slipped on her sleeping bag and fell off the platform. Luckily she fell only 10 feet (3.05 m) onto branches, but cracked some ribs and suffered back problems for a year. Another climber lost his grip on a traverse line and his safety rope cinched his waist, causing him to vomit, have breathing difficulties, and pass out while being rescued. And yet, Cascadia Forest Defenders claimed that of the thousand or so treesitters defending forests in Washington, Oregon and California since 1998, most suffered no accidents, although some accidents had resulted in death.

Tangent and I parked a box of food at an intersection of logging roads, where another blue tarp provided shelter. A sign nailed to a post announced Rainbow Kitchen. Other signs said: "Love works best" and "No animals eaten here."

"Want some coffee?" asked a young man wearing the skull of a small mammal around his neck. He smiled with straight white teeth as he stirred the coffee. Many of the treesitters had straight white teeth, I noticed. Peeking inside the pot, I could tell the coffee grounds were recycled. "No thanks," I said. Bags of dry bread and pesto passed from hand to hand. I declined that too. Talk settled on building another road barricade. Tangent didn't think it was a good idea. The women did. Decisions at Fall Creek were supposed to be made by consensus, although some decisions had been unilateral.

Tangent and I took our leave to refuel more treesits. En route we passed an ambulating treesitter. Tangent reminded him not to piss in the road. In the middle of it, a Douglas-fir seedling basked in the sun, ringed by small rocks. Elsewhere, said Tangent, feces and left-over food were buried in the logging roads to break them up. How to care for the environment was a matter of perspective.

After the last food delivery, Tangent invited me to visit the village shrine. We left the village proper and followed a foot trail of sorts. It led us over logs and stumps, which Tangent said marked scenes of former confrontation with loggers. An effective strategy for treesitters under attack, he said, was dropping spoonfuls of feces from their platforms. I imagined Tangent would be resourceful under such conditions. He said he had wanted to study counselling in college but found activism more rewarding.

Forest
Defender
climbing
with simple
gear

We pursued the trail that now only Tangent could discern. Coming upon a small clearing, we stopped. Tangent crouched down while I walked up to it—a six-foot-tall (1.8 m), curvaceous stump. Its twisted torso displayed a span of shoulders at the top and a burl below for a butt. The headless torso pooled water in its neck like a baptismal font. A small daisy graced a shoulder and shells, feathers, and jewelry adorned its feet.

Tangent said they called her Venus de Milo after her shapeliness. "At one time there was stuff all over her and I removed it," he said. "Word got back to town and people were angry that I did that. They said I had no right to remove their prayers. I said it wasn't right to cover her up like that." His last defence was communication with Venus herself, who, he said, had asked him to remove the clutter of holy objects.

I looked again at the anomaly for anything that might indicate it could communicate. But all I could perceive was the remainder of a tree that perhaps had snapped in a storm, or been logged, and the living wood of the stump had continued to grow upward. Tangent gazed upon the relic while I photographed it. Then we left.

Returning to Rainbow Kitchen, we passed the newly formed barricade crew. A young man with a small pickaxe was hacking at the road. A young woman dressed in a T-shirt and underwear was hauling rocks with her hands. Nearly two feet of forest debris had been piled across the road since we stopped by for breakfast. As Tangent escorted me to the village exit, he said treesitters get discouraged when the Forest Service bulldozes their hard work. Some leave, but some persevere, which is the mainstay of activism.

A year earlier I had attended the Nineth Annual Western Forest Activists Conference in Ashland, Oregon. I listened to tree village activists from Oregon and Washington speak about "Not your Grandma's Tactic Anymore." A twenty-something from the North Winberry treesit in Willamette National Forest captured my attention. She called herself Thunder.

When first arriving at North Winberry, she said she traversed a line between two trees in the middle of the night. Before that, she had travelled, worked for a year, and completed college. She had first wanted to become a physician to join Doctors Without Borders. But she decided to pursue her own college program instead—a mix of biology, political science and cross-cultural studies. She had prepared herself well for treesitting.

"Treesitters save forests," boomed Thunder. For a small-bodied female, she spoke with the force of conviction. "We put our lives on the line to hold off the chainsaw, hoping, number one, that zero cut is passed into law. But government processes are not always final and salvage riders are often tacked onto bills. Number two, we stall destruction, hoping that our presence gains time, time to unmask the atrocities, time to unmask the unjust laws. . . .

"We provide time to shed light on consumer trends that are changeable habits. We want people to understand that each thing you do in your lives affects the forest. The United States does not need to suck the Earth dry. We do not need to skin her for minerals. We do not need to suck up her oil, or cut down her appendages for wood. We are people who can choose to consume less, recycle more, invest in alternative energies. We can change political processes."

Thunder explained how, less than a year after the initial occupation of Fall Creek, the North Winberry treesit in the Winberry watershed got established. First came a platform in the tree called Life, and then platforms in the trees Glisten and Sorrow. Platforms were made from recycled plywood and parked on either static lines or webbing—not nailed into trees. Since the 1980s, platforms had evolved from 4 x 8 feet (1.2 x 2.4 m) units into "donuts" wrapped around tree trunks, providing rooms for eating, sleeping, playing guitar, reading books, and hanging out, literally.

Someone in the audience asked about her best and worst experiences while treesitting. She said the best experience in the trees was "just breathing—the wind constantly touches your face. When you live in the trees, you can't help but notice there's a life force that cannot be defined. It works every moment and flows all around you, throughout you, within itself, and that's something you can't read about or define. The fact that Nature is something that's a word is even amazing to me. The fact that you can be a part of Nature is amazing to me. So once you feel that power, then you're affected the rest of your life, and you can't ever not think about what happens on the ground. You can never not think about what you consume. You can never not think again about where you step every day. . . .

"The worst experience was my personal wondering at when the forest is going to be saved. Because you have a lot of time to stop and wonder. There have been efforts to remove treesitters from Fall Creek—drastic efforts. They have been harassed by endless ways of noise invasion. They've had huge searchlights flashed on them for days on end to try and keep them awake and disoriented, hoping they're not falling out of the trees but coming down of their own will. Didn't happen, but they have done everything they could think of to get people out of the trees. At North Winberry, we are in an area that is not under closure. It is legal for us to be there for 14 days, so that's all we stay, and then we just rotate."

I scanned the faces of people in the audience. Many expressed awe. I felt awe too. When you're twenty-something in the 21st century you may not have a mortgage or a family to support, but you do have a planet at risk.

Several months after my visit to Fall Creek, in October 2001, I stopped in for coffee at the Morning Glory Cafe. I noticed a handwritten bulletin tacked to a wall. It read: "Home of tree village unit 36 is cancelled, along with units 37 and 42. Help is needed to haul out gear, supplies and trash."

I checked in with Tangent by email when I got home. He replied that a lot had happened since we walked together through Fall Creek: "Fifty-one acres (20.6 ha) at Fall Creek have been saved, whooppee! It was due to the red tree vole surveys. The village where you seen the sits has been saved. The last I have heard is that they have more tree vole surveys goin' down and there will be more acreage buffered out for the voles. Anywho, November yes, I was planning on being back by then, don't know currently, things are always up in the air with me ya know. . . ."

Discovery of this forest species at risk in units of public forests for sale was a legal way to stop the logging. The red tree vole lives in the Pacific Northwest forest canopy of old-growth and is prey for the endangered northern spotted owl.

I called the Willamette National Forest District Ranger to confirm. He said treesitters had submitted red tree vole nest samples to the Forest Service, who verified the nests. Thirty-five active red tree vole nests and 25 inactive ones were confirmed in the Clark timber sale—the location of the Fall Creek treesit. Each group of active nests required a 10-acre (4-ha) buffer to protect the vole's habitat. I asked the ranger how the treesitters found more nests than the Forest Service. He said they did not have a protocol to identify 100 percent of the nests. "We start from the ground and look up, then we climb. They climb the trees. It appears that in the canopy you have a better view."

About a month later, I attended the Umpqua Action Camp. I had been told that treesitters organized action camps for strategizing, sharing skills and general inspiration, so I wanted to go.

I picked up my guide outside the office of Cascadia Forest Defenders in Eugene. Thistle (a pseudonym of a pseudonym) packed the backseat of my car with tree climbing gear. I drove south to the Umpqua National Forest, near Roseburg. On the way we talked about treesitting at Fall Creek. He told me about the time when the women kicked out the men from the trees because of their verbal abuse, and that the women held an all-female treesit for a month. This action was done by consensus. The men who were kicked out of the trees set up the Red Cloud Thunder barricade. That was not done by consensus. Perhaps Red Cloud Thunder believed in its own mandate. I had read that the early treesitters at Fall Creek named their campaign after Chief Red Cloud—the warrior chief of the Oglala Lakota who expelled the US Cavalry from his homeland.

Thistle seemed to be a gentle person. He said he was a glass artist and musician who donated his money to Cascadia Forest Defenders. He would be content to earn $800 a month to live and defend the forests, he said. Cascadia Forest Defenders get grants to keep the office open, but nobody gets paid.

We arrived at Umpqua in the early evening. Camp was being set up in the forest primeval. I set up my tent in the outskirts of the main community. It was getting colder, being a November night in the forest. I got inside my sleeping bag to warm up while the others made a fire. Listening to the rise and fall of voices, I fell asleep.

The next morning I awoke to the expletives of a young woman talking about the poor quality of tree village food. "That's all there was to eat," she went on, "just lettuce, apples and sunflower seeds." She called her parents when she started to convulse. At the hospital, staff confronted her about treesitting. She came for medical help, she retorted, and they were nice after that. Another successful stand-off for the forest.

I joined the campfire with a supply of peanut butter and oatmeal to share. Treesitters were delighted. Generally, I did what I could to be helpful, often wondering at their acceptance of me—a middle-aged woman wearing clean jeans without holes and a tidy jacket, often toting a notepad in my pocket, and driving an old Ford Escort with bumper stickers hailing the rights of snow and skate boarders (my teenaged daughter's sentiments).

For breakfast we shared food. After eating, some washed their faces with peels of grapefruit—the use of herbs and other natural remedies being preferred or necessitated. Then a circle was called to discuss the day's activity—sharing skills about how to survey for red tree voles.

With the day's action plan decided by consensus, we picked up gear and headed into the forest. I noticed that not everyone was prepared to climb trees. Some were organizers who stayed on the ground and others had been climbers who quit. A young man told me how he got stuck in a "pod" hanging between two trees for 36 hours during a winter storm; he said he would never treesit again but was committed to forest defence.

While treesitters climbed trees, the rest of us helped as we could. I mostly watched from the road. By noon, two locations for canopy surveys were found. Tree vole debris had been cited on the lower branches of Douglas-firs. Red tree voles eat the flesh of fir needles and discard the needle cores. They use the remnants and twigs to make nests in the higher canopy.

A group of us on the ground peered upward to glimpse vole debris. Thistle emerged with his crossbow and arrow. He shot a line as high as he could into the canopy, aiming for a thick horizontal limb to cross over and drop the line to the ground. The shot succeeded. The line was tied to a climbing rope and hauled back over the limb. The other end of the rope was tied to the base of the tree. A young woman offered to climb. She ascended without much equipment—no fancy harness or helmet— and reached the branch with tree vole debris. A support branch broke. "I'm really stuck," she yelled. But in a few moments she figured out the next step, swinging around the trunk to gain another foot-hold.

Just then, a car with two young men drove up. I could tell that they were one of us. "Unit 12 is not going to be auctioned," said the driver (we were surveying unit 12). "We need to survey unit 4 instead—that one will be for sale next month."

When the tree climber exclaimed that she found vole scat, we shouted back, telling her to come down. No one seemed disappointed or frustrated by the abrupt change of plans. Dogged persistence was assumed.

Time passed after the Umpqua Action Camp and I lost connection with Cascadia Forest Defenders. A news report in 2003 rekindled my interest. A wildfire had broken out in the Fall Creek watershed. As acres burned in the Clark timber sale, treesitters were evacuated, according to the Eugene office of the Willamette National Forest. But some treesitters remained, according to the Eugene office of Cascadia Forest Defenders.

I called the office and spoke with a treesitter who answered the phone. She said fire never reached the village at Fall Creek, but there had been ongoing problems with "oppressive behaviour." A lot of treesitters were uneducated about certain forms of oppression, she said. In April 2003, a regional "anti-oppression" policy was issued, and most Cascadia Forest Defenders accepted it. It was an evolving policy, she said, which at the time, included the following:

> The anti-oppression agreement is based in both theory and experience. As a collective, we are committed to the desire to not recreate or perpetuate oppressive relationships of the dominant society. Examples of these oppressive relationships include racism, sexism, classism, heterosexism, homophobia, ageism, ableism, colonialism, speciesism, etc. . . . The Earth First! movement has traditionally been a white, male-dominated space, reinforcing patriarchal behaviours that reflect the dominant society. Violence such as rape and sexual assault, as well as other physical, verbal, and emotional abuses that manifest themselves in social domination/subordination are prevalent throughout the dominant patriarchal society. Our goal is to inspire the radical environmental momentum to be as free from these oppressions as possible. . . . If one accepts the reality of oppression in our lives, then coming to an agreement against oppression does not deny anarchy; rather, it reinforces a commitment to the autonomy and safety of all living beings. . . .

The treesitters at Fall Creek did not agree to the anti-oppression policy, she said. It was assumed that they didn't like having a policy imposed from the outside. Consequently, Cascadia Forest Defenders officially separated from the Fall Creek treesit by June 2003. The treesitters who remained at Fall Creek moved to other parts of the forest. They vowed not to leave until the timber sale was cancelled for good. Their policy was: "No Compromise—Not Willing to Trade Trees for Trees." Perhaps they knew the forest's history.

In 1992, Oregon Natural Resource Council and its coalition first appealed the logging of the 94-acre (38-ha) Clark timber sale. They claimed it threatened the northern spotted owl, and the Forest Service lacked an adequate plan to maintain its population.

The 1994 Northwest Forest Plan called for protecting about 7 of 8 million acres (2.8 of 3.2 million ha) of remaining old growth forest on federal lands in range of the owl. About one million acres (404,685 ha) would be available for logging. When the Plan became law, the Clark timber sale was included in the one-million acres for logging.

Oregon Natural Resource Council and coalition again appealed the Clark timber sale, because the Forest Service did not survey for forest species at risk, which was required by the Plan. In 1999, the court ruled that surveys were mandatory and logging should not proceed until surveys were done and protection buffers applied.

In 2002 the size of the Clark timber sale reduced to 29 acres (11.7 ha) due to finding red tree voles that required habitat buffers. A timber industry coalition filed suit, claiming that acres reserved for logging by the Plan were unlawfully conserved.

In 2004, the requirement to survey and manage forest species at risk was removed from the Plan. Protection for the red tree vole in the Clark timber sale was cancelled and the forest went up for sale again. Oregon Natural Resource Council and coalition again filed suit.

In 2005, I wondered what had become of the Fall Creek tree village. Sifting through my contacts, I found a treesitter willing to guide me into the forest. He was wanting to take down the ropes left in the trees and "clear old energies" at the foot of the shrine. Our trip was set and reset, but we could never connect because there were always more forests for him to protect.

I contented myself with reading back issues of Cascadia Forest Defenders' *Green Canopy* newsletter. Treesitters reported to have slept on the ground around Venus. Some had heard her sing:

> Tonight I lay beside her, listening, both of us deep in thought, sap covered. The noise of whispers through the silence is louder than anyone can imagine and I sit up in my sleeping bag and stare into the indigo night. The stars stare back, millions of years old and each of them completely unconcerned with my small existence. . . I sat for a while and listened to the wind song. There is a restlessness to the sound, a sadness and a strength. Freeing myself from my sleeping bag, I pulled on my shoes. I had decided to walk up to base camp to see what everyone else thought of this crazy opera that was whistling about us. Trance-like, I stumbled up to camp over fallen logs, moss and 700-year-old roots. For the second time that night I began to ponder just how small my twenty-something years of existence were to this world. Lost in my thoughts, it was only when I got to camp that I realized that it was completely silent. In the morning no one had heard it. No one. Since then I have heard similar tales. . . .

It's a common experience to feel small in a forest, but it's uncommon to feel empowered by it. When you're a twenty-something Forest Defender, you can feel small and empowered at the same time.

Venus de Milo

SHARON McCANN

§♦

Chapter Seven
BIG TREE HUNTERS
British Columbia

Perhaps twenty-something Randy Stoltmann also pondered his relationship to ancient trees, and was awed by their grandeur. In 1988 Randy and a friend discovered giant Sitka spruce trees in the Carmanah Valley of southwest Vancouver Island, BC. Campaigning with Western Canada Wilderness Committee, they protected the area from logging. In 1990, the BC government conserved it by declaring the lower Carmanah Valley a provincial park; in 1995, the Walbran and upper Carmanah Valleys were added. Today, the Carmanah Walbran Provincial Park, 16,450 hectares (40,648 acres) in size, features 800-year-old spruce trees and 1000-year-old cedars in an intact temperate rainforest of global significance. Visitors come from all over the world to experience what is called the "Green Cathedral."

Randy published three books about the BC wilderness and big trees. In 1986, at 24 years of age, he established BC's Big Tree Registry. Sadly, eight years later Randy died on a mountaineering trip at the age of 32. By the time I looked into the Registry, in 2007, Randy had not yet been outdone for having found the most record trees. He had registered 42 record trees, of which 12 still held top place for their species.

I had long wanted to go on a big tree hunt. I imagined it to be risky but well rewarded by the awe of grandeur. Being a woman, I also wanted to understand what motivated men to find the biggest tree.

A careful review of the BC Big Tree Registry led me to contact Ralf Kelman. As of 2007, Ralf Kelman came in second behind Randy for the number of big trees nominated—a total of 40. Ralf tree hunted in the Lower Mainland, and represented the Lower Mainland in the BC Big

Tree Committee. He and Shaun Muc once held the record for the world's biggest poplar, a black cottonwood that has since split and fallen. As of 2007, by himself and with others, Ralf had nominated more black cottonwoods (12) and more Douglas-firs (7) than anyone else in BC. He and D. Yochim found the tallest recorded Douglas-fir in BC, measuring 94.30 metres (310 ft), in the Coquitlam watershed, east of Vancouver. I learned a lot about Ralf's passion for big trees when we spoke on the phone.

"Why do I do tree hunting?" he pondered in response to my question. "Because they're there. I just feel the sense of them being out there. And I sometimes feel as if they want me to find them. You know what? I've saved a lot of trees, not as many as some people, but I have felt driven to go somewhere. I've run around measuring trees to document them, and then two months later I find out there's a logging road being rammed in."

"How did it all start," I asked.

Ralf said he became interested in big tree hunting when he felt the need to break away from what had preoccupied him in the city. Ralf was also a conceptual artist. His career began by drawing homes for the upscale and painting city night scenes, which sensitized him to urban light. He went on to light sculpting, creating multi-media works such as lighting up part of Vancouver with road flares, which led him to activism as the first lighting environmentalist in North America. For five years in the early 1970s Ralf traveled throughout North America by bus, living on small honorariums and art council grants, decrying light pollution in urban centres and promoting task lighting and daylight in office workplaces. In 1976 the Vancouver Art Gallery exhibited "Lite Probe," which artistically documented Ralf's inquiry into urban light.

"My father was a real outdoorsman," Ralf continued. "He explored the mountains. That's when I got my first taste—going to places where few humans go. I loved being outdoors and loved hiking." While hiking a trail at the University of BC endowment lands, he came upon a big stump. "I was blown away by the size of the stump," he said. He realized that stumps provided an appreciation of the size of trees in the original forests. So he went looking for stumps: "I mapped them and photographed them, and I would tell people that I found these incredible stumps."

After a summer of stump hunting, Ralf decided to look for big trees. "One day in 1989 I followed a trail that leads up to Grouse Mountain. I got this feeling to push through—I get these premonitions that propel me through the bush. And as I'm turning, I see the top of a big tree. It was impressive, so I said to myself, 'Let's go.' I climbed up a slope aways and I could see this big trunk. I got up to it—a magnificent Douglas-fir.

Ralf Kelman
beside super
stumps in
Stanley Park

It was my first big tree. To me it was huge. I was so excited about this tree.

"I went home and read the book by Randy Stoltmann—it had recently come out—*Hiking Guide to the Big Trees of Southwestern British Columbia*. I called him about my discovery. We got together and went out. When I showed him the tree, he said he'd seen bigger. He wasn't that excited about it. He said, 'That's nice, but what else is here?' We bounded up the slope. It was my first day out with Randy and I got the tree searching bug. Randy was the guru of big trees. I haven't stopped since. I've actually found trees without seeing them, once I get going. I've changed my lifestyle just so I could get out there. I think they like me. I go back after I've saved them. I register to help save them."

"Why do you call it tree searching?" I asked.

"Because tree hunting sounds like game hunting and I've been a vegetarian my whole life."

Ralf told me about a trip he was lining up in the Coquitlam watershed, a site filled with 300-foot-tall (91.4-m) Douglas-firs. There's a gorge, he said, that drops hundreds of feet. "Nobody's been down in it, but we've skirted it forever. This one might be extreme tree searching."

The tree search was planned for next month, May 2007, and Ralf invited me to come along. He warned me that it would lead us down very steep slopes. If we found a big tree, he said my name would be on the record, so I was keen to go. But I sensed that Ralf would lead me into an adventure for which I should have no expectations, and may not be prepared.

Historically, the Coquitlam watershed was off-limits to the general public, being a drinking water supply area for the Greater Vancouver Regional District. When the district set up a stewardship program, they admitted community stakeholders. Because Ralf was a Big Tree Committee member, he could make a date with the watershed forester, Derek Bonin, to gain entry. Derek had gone before with Ralf into the area, and they found a big Doug-fir that Ralf named after Derek—the Bonin Giant. In 2007, the Bonin Giant held second place in the Douglas-fir category of the BC Big Tree Registry, measuring 65.84 metres (216 ft) tall, with a 12.5-metre (41-ft) circumference and a 21.95-metre (72-ft) crown spread.

In May I picked up Ralf in downtown Vancouver and we drove to Derek's office at the Greater Vancouver Regional District. En route, Ralf explained how he surveyed for big trees. He used aerial photos, forest cover maps showing height, and Google Earth on the Internet. He was always on the lookout, he said. He did not drive. When he travelled by city bus or someone else's vehicle, he did windshield surveys. If you really want to find a big one today, he said, you have to get on the ground and soldier through devil's club to where the loggers dared not go. (The Latin name for devil's club is *Oplopanax horridus*. It grows up to 9 feet [2.7 m] tall and defends itself with spikes up to one centimetre long on its stem and spines beneath its leaves.) I hoped we wouldn't have to soldier through devil's club.

Arriving at the district office, Ralf introduced me to Derek. We were a unique crew: a registered professional forester who was tall, thin and trim; Ralf—short, thin and sporting a pony-tail beneath his tuque; and myself, feeling out of place. Without delay, we were shown to a government vehicle. With Derek in the driver's seat and Ralf in the front, we headed northeast through the city to the Coquitlam watershed via Pipeline Road.

As Pipeline Road began to parallel the Coquitlam River, Ralf recalled how he had become aware of the potential of the Coquitlam watershed for growing big trees. From Burke Mountain, he said, you get a great view of the valley and Coquitlam Lake. From the vantage of the mountain top, he had watched clouds floating through the tops of giant firs in the watershed. He rented a plane twice with another tree searcher and flew over the area. He took buses to the end of the line and scrambled up to the ridge tops.

We arrived at the watershed security gate and drove through. Continuing on the road, Derek drove to the security office and parked. He went to the office to speak with staff, and Ralf and I followed. Inside, posted on a wall was a map of where we were going. The topographic lines showed significant elevation change. Derek pointed to our destination—the confluence of Coquitlam River and How Far Creek. The name of the creek caught my attention. Whenever I found myself asking "how far" on a hike, I was always exhausted. One of the staff remarked to me that Derek hiked like a gazelle. I began to worry.

We returned to the vehicle and Derek continued to drive upward, into the foothills of the Coast Mountains. Driving on Coquitlam Mainline Rd. East, we passed trucks carrying rock blasted from a quarry to restore the dam that had turned Coquitlam Lake into a water reservoir—one of three for Greater Vancouver. "Inbound, Coquitlam east, 5 K," said Derek on the radio phone to oncoming truckers. Passing by Cedar Creek, Ralf pointed to a cedar grove where he had measured the biggest cedar stump he had ever found—57 feet (17.4 m) in circumference.

"I have a thing about stumps," he remarked. Derek remained focused on the road while I looked out the window at the trees and trucks. Ralf did not elaborate. He had already told me that he thought super stumps should be recorded in the BC Big Tree Registry. He called it forest archeology. The stumps are all we have left of the great forests, he reasoned, and stumps are also disappearing. So far, the BC Big Tree Committee had not adopted a super stump category.

We reached a bridge and crossed over Coquitlam River and parked on a side of the road. We got out and looked down at the river rushing into a canyon. It really would be a steep descent to tree search, I realized. Derek explained the geography of the area. At the end of the last Ice Age, glaciers had moved through these U-shaped valleys and scoured them out, creating mountains with vertical and smooth granite sides. Several hundred inches of rain fell per year, growing big trees

Ralf scanned the vista for the big Doug-firs that had been calling to him. He took a photograph and said with modest excitement, "The adventure begins." Ralf said he aimed to find a Douglas-fir taller than the tallest Douglas-fir in North America—the Brummitt Fir in the Coos Bay area of Oregon, measuring 329 feet (100.3 m) tall. Even though we were venturing into the semi-wild, previously logged Coquitlam watershed, Mother Nature still offered big tree searchers a grand prize.

Derek drove some more and parked along the road. We got out of the vehicle and looked down the slope. As Derek donned his caulk boots, he said it might get wet down there near the creek. I noticed the spikes on the soles of his boots; they would give a good grip on wet wood. I looked down at my hiking boots without spikes. I would avoid stepping on wet downed trees, I decided. Ralf looked at his running shoes and complained about getting his feet wet.

Ralf and I packed water and snacks in our bags, and then Derek locked the vehicle, leaving his one granola bar on the seat. Noticing that, my apprehension increased.

Facing the slope going down, Derek parted the bush and disappeared. Ralf and I followed. This was real bushwacking, but it felt like bush diving. Forcing my body downward into prickly branches demanded steadfast will power. After about a half-hour of this, we came to a small clearing. Ralf asked Derek to measure a western redcedar with his laser. Ralf said he depended on others to measure his trees: "Precision with some species like black cottonwood and Sitka spruce is a nightmare. It's not something you can do quickly, and then somebody will argue with you. It's a big production." Derek measured the cedar at 67.5 metres (223 ft). "We don't have a champion," announced Ralf.

We continued downward. The bush thinned out and the number of trees increased. I guessed that the loggers had reached their limits of what they would fell and haul upwards on a steep slope. The next big Douglas-fir we found had bark so thick I could put my entire hand into one of its fissures. Derek asked me to hold the end of the tape measure at breast height against the tree. He walked along a fallen log with the tape to get a clear view of the tree's base and top to site it with his clinometer. He explained that where the forest is dense, it's easier to get an accurate measurement using a clinometer and tape measure. With a laser, the challenge is maintaining a clear line of sight for the laser beam to strike the tree without interference from tree branches and bush. Derek measured the Douglas-fir at 88 metres (290 ft) tall. Ralf said finding Douglas-firs taller than 270 feet (82.3 m) is a thrill, and finding any 300 feet (91.4 m) tall is rare. Derek said taller trees would likely be growing further down near the creek.

We continued to descend. I stepped on logs that crumbled beneath my feet, fell onto a mossy hollow, nearly bouncing and nearly swearing out loud about this mainly male endeavour. To date, only a few women had nominated trees for the registry, and none claimed champions.

When we could see and hear the running water of How Far Creek, Ralf and Derek located a Doug-fir to measure. It stood in a small grove of three really tall Doug-firs that had withstood large woody debris deposited from the swollen creek. It measured 84.5 metres (279 ft) and was not a champion. Ralf paused for some moments to gawk at the three trees. I watched Ralf as he stood in rapt attention. Then he said we were in the presence of greatness. I looked up and down the trees and wondered what he beheld. We had reached the creek and measured trees but found no record. I was tired and disappointed.

Derek said it was time to return. I looked up the slope to assess. It would be more difficult to bushwhack upward than downward. The winter snow load had bent the bush downward. We would have to lunge forward into prickly stems. No sooner had I determined the challenge than Derek had already begun to sprint upwards. Ralf and I followed. My strategy was pretending to swim upstream with a breaststroke.

When we reached the road, Ralf looked down at the big trees that had lured him for so long. "This was a real grind," he said. He looked at me and waited for a comment. I just looked down. Getting back in the vehicle, I complained that we didn't find the Big One. Derek said we found "a highly productive ecosystem." Ralf said you just don't find such tall Douglas-firs in a grove like that anymore.

As we drove out of the watershed, Ralf pointed out the sites of the record big trees he had found, and the general location of the Big One that continues to lure him. He said, "It sticks out its top at me and says 'Ha-ha' every time I pass it by."

Those who are not inclined to go on extreme tree searches can find at least one BC champion tree within easy access. The Douglas-fir world champion is only 30 minutes by car from Port Renfrew and then a short distance on a logging road. A 10-minute hike on a fairly clear trail leads to the Red Creek tree. Nominated by A.C. Carder, it's not as tall as the Oregon Brummitt Fir, but it's the biggest, with all measurements considered: 73.80 metres (242 ft) tall, 13.28 metres (43 ft 7 inches) circumference, and a crown spread of 22.80 metres (75 ft). Most likely the historical average annual precipitation on Vancouver Island's southwest coast contributed to its size.

Giant western redcedars grow in this region too. Randy Stoltmann had found several big ones northwest of Carmanah Walbran Provincial Park. But the reigning BC champion western redcedar to-date was found by Maywell Wickheim in 1988. Variously called the Cheewhat Giant or the Cheewhat Cedar, it's considered to be Canada's largest tree.

Like Ralf, Maywell noticed stumps. It was a western redcedar stump at the Smokey Point rest stop on Interstate 5, north of Everett,

Washington that gave Maywell a clue of the species' potential. Showcased since 1971, the stump measures 6.1 metres (20 ft) in diameter. When a fire burned in the standing tree's hollow base in 1893, it measured 61 metres (200 ft) tall. In 1916 the tree was topped and an archway cut through its stump. In 1922 the stump was cut from its roots and set upon a concrete base. By 1939 the stump had cracked, was taken apart, glued together, and moved to the highway, where Crown Prince Olav and Princess Martha of Norway drove through it. Today it's roofed and its history posted beside it. Maywell had measured the stump at least three times over the years.

For the record, Maywell measured his Cheewhat cedar to be 58.52 metres (192 ft) tall with a circumference of 18.59 metres (61 ft). But BC's Big Tree Registry reported the Cheewhat's size based on the measurements of American big tree hunter Robert Van Pelt: 55.5 metres (182 ft) tall, 18.34 metres (60 ft, 2 in) circumference. According to Robert, an American western redcedar in Washington's Olympic National Park is the biggest. He measured the Quinault Lake Cedar to be 53 metres (174 ft) tall with a 18.66-metre (61 ft, 3 in) circumference. With all measurements considered (the American Forests point system adds circumference in inches, height in feet and average diameter of the crown), Robert claimed the Quinault Cedar to have 920 American Forests points and the Cheewhat 917.

There were causes for measurement differences. Robert measured with a Criterion 400 survey laser. At the time, the US Forest Service considered this tool to be extremely accurate; however, it required specialized training, being designed for forestry professionals, and cost US $17,000 in 2007. Maywell measured with tools suggested by American Forests. For the circumference, Maywell used a tape measure standing at the tree's centre, measuring at 4.5 feet (1.4 m) above ground. Both Robert and Maywell agreed it's difficult to be exact in circumference measurement because giant trees can have irregular trunk shapes and stand on uneven ground. But Robert claimed that a tape measure can inflate the size because a giant tree trunk is not perfectly round.

Another Cheewhat measurement of contention was tree height. Robert sketched all the trees in his book, *Forest Giants of the Pacific Coast,* where he published his measurements. He claimed accuracy by using his laser. Maywell used a surveyor's transit. He said he measured the Cheewhat's tree height with many people, including a forest industry engineer, all of whom confirmed his measurement. There was only one small spot on the ground from where to view the tallest treetop, Maywell claimed. "The picture he sketched of the Cheewhat doesn't show the highest point."

Given the uneven ground and irregularity of giant tree trunks, Robert asserted that wood volume of the main stem (and the large resprouted, or reiterated trunks) is a more accurate indicator of size. To his credit, Robert measured wood volumes of the cedars, and found the Quinault Cedar to have more wood volume (500 cubic metres) than the Cheewhat (449 cubic metres).

With all measurements considered, an important qualitative difference between the two cedars was not considered crucial in the competition. Robert admitted that the Cheewhat Cedar is very healthy, while the Quinault Cedar is barely alive, having only a 2-foot (.61-m) wide strip of living bark that ascends the trunk and travels up one of its reiterated trunks. Regardless of measurements, the determination of which appears to be a matter of opinion, these ancient cedars must be seen to be appreciated. Their wood is so resistant to decay that when the main stem dies, new trunks resprout to create magnificent towers.

I met Maywell Wickheim for the first time at a truck scale turn-off on the Trans Canada Highway, Vancouver Island. I parked at a commuter lot nearby, threw my pack in the back of Maywell's dark green suburban, and sat behind him in the back seat beside Katy and Mike. Dick was the driver. We rumbled westward on the Cowichan Valley Highway. Our destination—the Cheewhat Cedar.

As we rumbled down the road, often swerving around potholes, I mostly observed the back of Maywell's head, which was covered in light brown hair and a cap. Maywell was talkative. He told stories about working for MacMillan and Bloedel, whose rise to the largest timber corporation in Canada corresponded with Maywell's logging career from 1939 to the early 1960s. Instead of going to high school, Maywell had to work to support the family. He felled his first tree at age 13. Once upon a time when he was felling a tree on the upslope, it fell on a log on the downslope and rolled toward Maywell, who tried to escape its path but got pinched between the log and a tree. Two vertebrae were crushed and he was hospitalized for six months. On better days he enjoyed log rolling. He also worked as a log scaler, high rigger, timber cruiser, log boom tower, donkeyman, and chokerman. In later years Maywell took to voluntarily clearing trails in the San Juan Ridges on the southwest of Vancouver Island.

Maywell found the Cheewhat Cedar and Maywell maintained the trail to the tree, clearing it in the spring after winter storms had passed. The tree stands within the Pacific Rim Park, but staff don't maintain the trail because it's an unofficial route. If a trail was built, it might encourage uncontrolled access to the West Coast Trail according to park staff, which would pose safety concerns. West Coast Trail hikers have met with all manner of accidents on the challenging route, and at times needed coast guard and helicopter rescues. A Canadian national park reserve, the Pacific Rim encompasses 511 square kilometres (197 sq. mi.) of land and ocean within three separate regions.

A spring day in 2007 was the first trail clearing to the Cheewhat Cedar for the year. The route to the Cheewhat led Dick toward Carmanah Walbran Provincial Park. Passing a sign to the park, he parked on a shoulder of the road, near ribbons fluttering on a bush. Such a signpost seemed odd to me for flagging a record tree, but the giant cedar is only a provincial record. Another oddity: The US has a national register of big trees, updated every two years by American Forests Association; the UK has a tree register for the British Isles; but Canada, a major global supplier of wood products, whose flag bears a maple leaf, keeps no big tree national registry. Does Canada take its abundance for granted? The Canadian Forestry Association honours National Forest Week and National Tree Day during the last week of September, although many Canadians may not even know about it.

As we tumbled out of the suburban to put on rain gear in the rain, Dick remarked, "A typical west coast day." Mike picked up the chainsaw and axe, Katy took the loppers, and Dick and I gripped gas containers. I asked Maywell how long to the tree—a typical question of mine.

"About an hour," he mumbled and headed quickly down slope into tall bush that had grown over a clearcut. Everyone else followed Maynard faster than I could keep my boots out of big puddles and not slip on wet blowdown. Log steps that had been set in place to stabilize the slope for hauling were now steps for a picturesque little waterfall. Trying to sidestep it, bush whacked me in the face. Bushwhacking is a matter of perspective; you can whack the bush or the bush can whack you.

It was mostly because I was paying attention to where I stepped on this cat track-and-backspar trail inside a 1987 clearcut that Dick and I got left behind. When we realized that we were lost, Dick and I poked around and ended up where he had parked the vehicle. By now my hiking boots were so wet they had filled up with about a half inch of water. We turned around and proceeded down the trail again. By the time we found Maywell, my boots had collected another half inch of water, and Mike had begun to chainsaw trees that had fallen over the trail. Maywell said they had waited several times for us and were surprised we got lost.

"You just look for where it's cleared," he said. "In about a month, I'll be leading a busload of hikers coming from the Sooke Regional Museum to see the tree." I remarked that this was quite a hike for the average museum-goer. He replied, "Even half-crippled seniors and three-year-olds make the trip." I couldn't tell if he was joking.

We continued forward into seven-inch pools of water on the trail. I had begun to estimate water depth, but not for any benefit. Western redcedar shingles abandoned by a poacher littered another stretch of trail. Three stretches of trail that followed needed knotted ropes for descent over granite and tree roots. Maywell took every challenge in stride. Sometimes he broke branches in our way and held them as if not to litter the garden.

Mike stopped to saw blow down on the trail and Maywell and I walked ahead. We found two more logs in the way, one on top of the other, and Maywell told me to stay put as he climbed over the logs into the forest. I leaned against a giant log, removed my boots one at a time and dumped out about a half a cup of water from each boot. I began to shiver. I wanted to hike back to the vehicle. I did want to see the tree, but I didn't want to clear trail anymore. I did care about the Cheewhat, but not as much as Maywell. I looked in my backpack for dry gloves, but they too were wet.

Mike arrived with his chainsaw, along with Katy and Dick. Then Maywell re-emerged from the forest. He declared that the Cheewhat had survived the winter storms. Relief broke through his brow.

Excited, we all powered forward. Maywell used the loppers to clear overhanging brush. A big cedar claimed the left side of the trail. It had been topped by natural forces but retained two spires that rose from its main trunk. I stopped to gawk at the spires. I had never seen such an old cedar before. Maywell said it was about 2500 years old. Continuing on the trail, he commandeered the chainsaw to cut more blowdown. The Cheewhat was 200 metres away, he said. I hiked ahead. As the trail bent to the left, I looked downslope and beheld it.

The cedar was so massive at its base, so rippled by the column-like roots of several trees growing from it, it looked like a castle. It must have been trees like this that had inspired the architecture of ancient civilizations. As I gazed upon the tree, I forgot it was raining. Above the canopy of several trees rooted in its buttress, the tree split into two spires that split again into five. I walked around the tree and stopped to observe how the tree had closed a wound. The giant looked to be in good health.

As I made my way around the Cheewhat, counting the trees and shrubs growing on it, I found myself repeating that this was the most beautiful tree I had ever seen. Completing the trip around the tree, I found Maywell leaning into the cave of a smaller cedar upslope, gazing upon his prize. Mike and Dick sat beside him. Katy took photos in the rain. Maywell said he had once drilled into the trunk of a fallen cedar nearby and counted the rings. Extrapolating, he estimated the Cheewhat to be about 3500 years old.

Cheewhat
Cedar,
Maywell
Wickheim
(left) and
friends

Dick watched as I circled the tree again and confirmed my count of 15-and-a-half, two-arm-span circumference around the Cheewhat. On the way around the tree, I passed not one but two official Pacific Rim National Park signs, proclaiming the tree as "part of Canada's natural heritage which is protected under the Canada National Parks Act," and requested that "you can help preserve this impressive natural wonder for our grandchildren" by not disturbing the soil, not climbing the tree, not taking a bit of bark, and respecting the nearby vegetation. The forest soil is shallow, and beneath it is clay, so even the big trees have shallow root systems.

After a time of resting and tree gawking, Maywell led us downslope from the Cheewhat to a felled cedar beside its stump. The end of the log had been chiseled. Maywell estimated the "canoe tree" had been abandoned 200 years ago. One of the common names for the western redcedar is canoe tree; it's considered the cornerstone of northwest coast native culture because of its many uses. According to local historians, of which Maywell was considered one by the Sooke Region Historical Society, the Nitinaht people chose cedar trees that, once felled, could be slid downhill. Maywell had found eight such canoe trees in this area.

Maywell told us that he had stumbled in these woods for a total of ten days looking for the champion. He found it with Angela Bailey, his secretary/bookkeeper for his business, Sooke Marine Industries. Before that, he had traipsed around the area for four years on several-day expeditions. He figured that the dense rainforest offered good growing conditions, that the steep slopes would protect big trees against wind damage, and the remoteness would protect them from logging. Rumours of big spruce tree sightings had also drawn him to the Carmanah Valley. He explored the valley by tracking down forest surveyor notes at offices of MacMillan Bloedel, and flying over it by plane.

What really motivated Maywell to find the Cheewhat Cedar was not its size. He said it was the continued felling of big old trees, without regard for saving the outstanding ones, or outstanding groves of them for future generations.

Being in the presence of this outstanding tree affected my perspective. We are not bigger than Nature. The life force of Nature is greater than us.

SHARON McCANN

ॐ

Chapter Eight
EAGLE TREES
Washington

S tanding on the lawn of a suburban home with a small flock of local
residents, I waited. It was a chilly November afternoon in 2004. To
keep warm, I began to amble. Sometimes I looked upward and
westward into the grey sky above the Pacific Ocean. I noticed others
doing the same. People who live on this narrow, six-mile peninsula of
Washington State's south coast must look up into the sky a lot, I
thought. Ocean Shores is said to be one of the best birding spots in the
state, with about 300 species recorded annually.

I set up a camera with a telephoto lens on a tripod on the lawn. A few
people sauntered over to check out my camera gear and chat. I met Don
and his wife Dalene. They had moved to Ocean Shores because of the
birds and water views, they said. They were also members of a local, ad
hoc group called the Concerned Citizens. The Concerned Citizens had
coalesced when eagle perch trees on residential lots were felled. Don and
Dalene were so concerned that they purchased the undeveloped lot #43
beside the property where we stood. They wanted to protect its eagle
nest tree, even though it was protected by law.

Don explained to me: "Bad storms can blow 70 to 100 miles (112 to
161 km) per hour here. If there are bunches of trees, the wind lifts over
them. If there is a single tree, the wind will blow the nest tree down. So
saving the trees is important to save the nest tree."

Movement near a truck parked on the driveway beside lot #43 caught
my attention. A clean-shaven, slightly balding, muscular man began to
change his clothes. Taking off his black cowboy hat and leather jacket,
Tim Brown donned camouflage overalls. Chuck Gibilisco, who worked

87

for the Washington Department of Fish and Wildlife (WDFW), gathered rope and cable from his truck. They had invited me to this event.

We spectators moved in around the truck. As Tim strapped on spurs and metal shin plates over his boots, Chuck explained that the spurs were sterilized to minimize infection to the tree, and that Tim used spurs as a last resort, when a tree had too much rot or weak points for safe climbing. He usually ascended trees by rope.

Then Tim attached two sets of thick, coiled rope to his hip and walked confidently a few feet into the wooded lot where a ladder leaned against an aging spruce. Tim took one step and then another on the rungs while his carabiners clanked against the ladder's metal frame. No one said a word as we watched him step upward.

Reaching the top rung of the ladder, Tim threw a rope around the mottled trunk. With the other arm, he reached around the trunk to catch the rope and clip it to his belt. Over and over he threw the rope that caught in spikes of broken limbs.

Tim grunted with more reach to catch the rope. After several more tries he caught it and clipped the rope to his belt. My mouth dropped open as I watched him lift off from the top rung of the ladder to shinny upward, digging spurs into the bark. He threw a second rope above his head around the trunk, clipped it to his belt, and shinnied up some more.

On the ground, Chuck said that Tim had invented this double flip-line technique. I bent back my head to watch Tim climb higher.

"The eagles are back!" Don shouted. About 10 feet (3.05 m) above the tree two eagles swooped low to check out the human in a hard hat climbing toward their nest. Eagles' nesting habits allow a few months only for installation of a camera in their nest. Egg laying begins in late March in Washington, and within 35 days, one or two eaglets hatch. By mid-July most eaglets fledge by using perch trees for flight training. By fall, adults and juveniles migrate to British Columbia and southeast Alaska. Adults return to their breeding territories by early winter.

Tim continued to climb. The eagle nest sat in branches about 90 feet (27.4 m) above ground in the 115-foot (35.05-m) tall spruce. My neck felt sore from looking upward and I felt cold from standing still. I left the group of spectators to walk around. I remembered the camera I had set up on the lawn and went to take photos of Tim's climb from a distance.

Photos taken and still cold, I wondered if I might find refuge in the home that hosted this event. I knocked on the front door. Chayce opened it and invited me indoors. Nearly as soon as I sat down she said, "It just broke my heart. . . . I cried big tears. I would've bought that tree. I should've bought the lot." Chayce was referring to a 150-year old perch tree that her new neighbour felled behind her house. The eagle pair had moved into lot #43 when she bought her home in 1995. She had considered buying lot #43 or the lot behind her house. But then she didn't, thinking the law protected perch trees.

What the state law protected was eagle habitat, while perch trees were negotiable. US federal law protected nest trees only, and eagles, eggs and eagle parts. Thanks to three acts of Congress (the Migratory Bird Treaty Act of 1918, the Bald and Golden Eagle Protection Act of 1940 and the Endangered Species Act of 1973) plus the ban of DDT, the bald eagle had made a comeback. By 1999 it was proposed to remove bald eagles from the list of threatened species, subject to creation of a national monitoring plan. Earlier in 1986, Washington State had relaxed its eagle management plans, replacing standard buffers of habitat protection with negotiated plans between landowners and WDFW. Landowners were now allowed reasonable use of their property; where lots were small, reasonable use could result in removal of perch trees.

Chayce continued her lament while I sat upon the sofa getting warm. "Where do babies learn to fly if they don't have perching trees?" she said. "You should see the babies when they jump out of the nest. Humans can learn a lot from those eagles." What could we learn, I wondered. I doubted we could learn that much.

Chayce invited me to her backyard deck, where she often sat to watch eaglets learn to fly from the perch tree that had been cut down in her neighbour's yard. As we stood on the deck, she said her neighbours had received approval to fell some perch trees on their property. But then they torched the slash, the smoke of which distressed the nesting eaglets. After some investigation, the Concerned Citizens concluded that the real threat to the eagles was poor guidance from the town and state. Burning slash disturbed the eaglets, they claimed. But the state wildlife biologist disagreed: Those eaglets were ready to fledge and were tolerant of people, having built their nest within a pre-existing settlement.

Chayce and I went outside to check on Tim's progress. We could hear Chuck and Tim communicating by cell phones. Tim approached the nest. "The camera is attached to the striped line," said Chuck to Tim. "The drill should have the right bit." Tim dug into his backpack for the tool while Chuck fleeced the back of his pickup for cable. Tim reached the nest. It looked about 4 feet (1.2 m) wide and 2 feet (.61 m) deep with a 6-inch (15.2 cm) centre depth, he said. Tim drilled a branch and screwed on the camera mount. The camera he attached was no bigger than a thumb, Chuck explained.

A TV was set up in the back of Chuck's truck. He grabbed cable hanging from the tree that Tim had hauled up and dropped. Chuck connected the cable to the TV and plugged in the TV to an outlet in the garage. The screen did not light up. We sighed. "Technical difficulties!" said Chuck, smiling like it was familiar. He fidgeted with the line. Then

Chuck to Tim: "We're on the air!" We clustered closer to the screen. All we saw was a big bowl of twigs. I had hoped to see more, like what I'd been told accumulates in eagle nests over time, such as cat collars, crow heads, small mammal skulls, fish bones, and eagle eggs never hatched.

Chuck told Tim to reposition the camera for a better view. "Can we include the house where the lady does housecleaning in the nude?" asked a spectator. Chuck said that would be the end of the WildWatch Cam program. The men chuckled. Our eyes riveted to the TV screen. We could see a tree branch framing the view of Grays Harbor, looking east from Ocean Shores. We could also see that Tim was clenching his jaw. I checked my watch. From the first moment of his ascent, three hours had passed.

Tim Brown climbing to eagle nest

Chuck to Tim: "There's a hammer in the bag to smack that short limb." Tim found the hammer and whacked the limb. Then he threw a baseball cap into the centre of the nest. Chuck told Tim when we could see on screen the centre of the nest and a background of sky and water.

Tim's job was done. I sighed in relief even though he had done all the work. On his way down the tree, he stapled cable to the trunk, using camouflage staples. Chuck said the camera cable would attach to a modem donated by the neighbour who felled the perch trees, and Chayce and her husband would be able to watch the eagles real time, all the time, on their TV. Internet viewers of WDFW's website would be able to watch the eagles real time too, but with images refreshed every 10 seconds.

Four hours after his ascent, Tim set foot on ground and wiped his brow of sweat.

Tim Brown
near eagle nest

Tim and Chuck launched the WildWatch Cam program in 1999 on behalf of WDFW. It was hoped that by making it possible for the public to view wildlife close-up that it would be better appreciated and protected. Birdwatching in particular was popular. In 2001, the U.S. Fish & Wildlife Service reported over 1.6 million birdwatchers, or 36 percent of the population 16 years and older, in Washington State.

Tim and Chuck decided that the program's first webcam would watch a pair of nesting eagles. The public loved raptors and eagles were accessible. Two-thirds of Washington's bald eagles nested on private land. For a live eagle webcam, the chosen nest had to be used consistently. And the nest must be near power lines for cable and modem. WDFW would reimburse the landowner for expenses. Tim would train and work with agency staff, donate 35 of his own cameras, his climbing skills, and experience with camera installation. He would also share his passion for wildlife.

Tim's passion had a history. As we strolled through McWhirter Park in Tim's hometown of Redmond, Washington, he told me all about it. The fall day was grey and cool but Tim dressed as usual—in a leather jacket, cowboy hat and cut-off jeans. He was talkative by nature. He talked to birds too as we followed the winding path through the trees. He pointed out the wildlife trees he had carved for the park. They looked so natural.

"Why did you do that?" I asked. "Doesn't Nature do that?"

Tim's reply was a long story: He had worked with biologists from the Forest Service and National Park Service to create wildlife habitat in public forests. Second-growth forests did not have all of the parts of a naturally aged stand, he said. For eagles, who need tall trees to nest and see their prey, Tim pruned dense canopies and girdled branches for perches. To mimic a lightning strike, he would cut a long vertical slit along a tree trunk to help birds excavate for insects.

"I want it to look natural," he said, stopping to admire one of his handcrafted snags. "I'm one of Nature's artists. I mimic what I see in Nature. I take advantage of the rot in a tree and take my axe and bust the heck out of it. If I leave chop marks or saw marks, it's a failure."

Clearly, Tim had a penchant for helping snags—dead standing trees—fulfill their destinies. Snags are classified into several stages of decline and five stages of decay for those that have fallen. Each stage attracts different wildlife. Birds, bats and squirrels like standing snags, while mammals, amphibians, and reptiles are attracted to downed logs.

"Some trees have 15 cavities in them," Tim continued, "and other trees have a hollow and a bear in one part and a woodpecker in another part of it at the same time. Some trees have nests in them at the top—it's endless. And then they might not have a nest for 50 years. When it was smaller and a short tree, it had robin nests in the bottom of it because the tree structure was close to the ground. When it got taller, those birds didn't use it anymore. Then raptors, goshawks or owls used nests in mid-canopy or two-thirds of the way down the canopy because the branch structure is far enough apart. Or eagles hung out in them because they used them as thermal protection, like an umbrella at night, to preserve their energy and hide from the wind."

Tim savoured the memories of his handcrafted trees as we strolled. I looked for more of them, but could not identify them because every stage of tree life in the park looked natural. Tim said he created 2000 techniques for building wildlife habitat, and built over a quarter million wildlife trees throughout North America. Awards followed from numerous federal, state and international agencies, and conservation groups.

Tim said he operated a tree service in Redmond. When homeowners asked him to take down hazard trees, he offered to shorten them instead. When he suggested making wildlife trees in Redmond's parks, the park operations manager agreed because science was proving it was a good idea for forest health. Before this time, a dead or dying tree in a greenbelt or park was thought to be contagious by spreading rots and fungi.

"It was also an economic thing," Tim said. The cost to cut down a big hazard tree was about $3000 in the 1990s. "Our cost to go in there and make it a wildlife tree and leave the log and lop off the branches was $350. They liked that price tag big-time. So when we did that and they saw that it looked natural, it saved the city thousands and thousands of dollars."

Tim had also worked in logging: "At first I thought clearcuts were necessary. But I didn't think that for very long. I did think it for a little while because that's what I was taught. Then I saw the big slash burns of all the stuff on the ground, what natural fires didn't burn because they kind of creep around here and burn there, and the trees survive, although some don't, depending on the severity of the fire, the ecosystem, the age of the stand, and so on. But when the slash burned, the stuff was so intense on the forest floor that it just cooked and over-burned.

"It was also painful to go to work and cut trees and watch animals flying out of them. So I started leaving trees that had any wildlife in them at all. Even if they weren't living in a tree at the time, I left it. I got in a lot of trouble with my boss or the companies I worked for. They wanted that tree for lumber. I said, 'Well, you know, I'm going to leave it. If you want to cut it, you go cut it, but I'm not.' I cut on the very steep terrain, so they couldn't cut those trees because I was both the rock climber and timber faller. So I left them and they're still there today. I have no regrets. When I educated the rest of the logging crew, they felt the same way. Pretty soon everybody started leaving trees around rivers and streams."

By the time Chuck and Tim installed a webcam in a cottonwood in Kent in February 2000, Garry and Loraine had been watching eagles nest for nine years in their backyard. By May, webcam viewers had watched egg laying, hatching and eaglet feeding. WDFW reported more than 6000 website log-ons daily. Hundreds of emails were received too, with the greatest response coming from seniors, people in hospital and home-schoolers. They wrote about the psychological and spiritual uplift as well as the educational value of watching eagles rear their young.

With the advent of the webcam, Loraine created the *Journal from Down Under* and linked it to Bravenet, a website blog. During the sixth season of eaglet watching, Loraine commented about "Our EagleCam babies, Freedom and Liberty"—the offspring of Star and Spirit:

> Yes they are so BIG now! They're just six weeks old now and only one-half way there. . . . Not near ready to fledge. There are lots of lessons to learn and life skills to start mastering. Freedom and Libby (short for Liberty) still need to learn to stand upright longer than they do, then there's branching (jumping back and forth, branch to nest and vice versa). . . how to prepare and tear food to eat it and . . . well they just have a long way to go still before fledging . . . . The BEST part is that we're all able to watch it all happen!

Spirit was the second mate of Star since nesting began in the cottonwood. In 2003 Spirit ousted the former male from the nest, but performed poorly in his parenting duties. Only one eaglet hatched and the other egg dissolved. Twenty-four hours later, the eaglet that did hatch died. By the next season, dad did a better job. Loraine reported in the *Journal from Down Under*:

> At daylight and as soon as the eggs were visible we noticed the hole had changed to a crack and at 7:08 a.m., the first little fluff ball fully emerged! Everyone has been on pins and needles and the million dollar question this year is, will he or won't he? We're speaking of Spirit. He has a lot of making up to do for his poor performance last year, as most of us witnessed.
>
> At that time, Spirit was given a number of names he needed to shed in a hurry before they became attached permanently to such a regal bird. Some EagleCam viewers and Bravenet visitors had very definite ideas as to what his name should be. We have to admit at times we couldn't disagree, yet at the same time, these are Bald

Eagles, our nation's prestigious symbol. We realize this earned heckling is somewhat due to the lack of knowledge humans have into the world of these majestic birds. We do have to understand, though, apparently there were reasons this male eagle was acting this way, and we just don't know what they were.

In the summer of 2005 I went to visit Loraine at her home. Soon after welcoming me inside, she told me about the four TVs throughout the house. The first season of eaglet watching had produced 556 six- and eight-hour videotapes. For this season she said she was trying to be conservative, and had recorded only 150 tapes so far. Loraine offered me tea in the kitchen where we sat to talk. Warm-hearted and enthusiastic, she quickly drew me into the story of an eaglet last year getting trapped in fishing line in the nest. She feared it would die because it couldn't exercise its wings, and its sibling had begun to pick on it.

When she spoke about the problem with WDFW, they were concerned, she said, but tended not to interfere with wild animals. I recalled Chuck telling me about this event. He had said that making a decision was tough: "Do we interfere or don't we? Do we try a management regime of some sort? Do we take this sickly eagle out of the nest and send it to a rehab clinic, and have to deal with the consequences of reintroducing it to the nest? Will it be a wild eagle in Washington ever? There's lots of interesting dilemmas that this webcam has created for us."

It was difficult as well for Loraine and the extended eagle webcam family. Loraine explained to me: "The difference here is the fact that the eagles are watched all over the world." As the story unfolded, the eagles themselves made a concerted effort to solve the problem. The fishing line loosened and the eaglet got free—only to be trapped again. Loraine said she called Chuck again, but he had gone home for the day. So she called a wildlife rehabilitation centre. An agent came out, observed the eaglet on a monitor, and confirmed: it was trapped. She reached Chuck who contacted Tim. On the day before Tim planned to climb the tree, the eagles had bit through the line and freed the eaglet. Tim climbed the tree to the nest anyway.

"Sure enough," said Loraine, "he brought down a softball-sized mass of line, hooks, twine, and lures. I don't know if anybody kept it or if he still has it. I wish I could have kept it. It's kind of a sentimental thing I guess because I watched the poor thing struggle."

Loraine invited me into her backyard wildlife sanctuary. It was certified by both the State of Washington and the National Wildlife Federation. She showed me the ponds and a stream that provided habitat for ducks and frogs and also watered the cottonwood eagle nest tree. I remarked that the tree stood close to the house. She said an eagle had once dropped a fish onto her mother-in-law's feet as she sat upon the patio. No matter—wildlife was welcome.

I noticed nest debris of feathers and fallen sticks littering the lawn. The feathers, cautioned Loraine, must be left alone by law. She said government officials send them to a depository where American Indians can request them for ceremonies. Mere possession of eagle feathers, body parts or nests, as well as cutting down a nest tree, bring stiff penalties under the Bald and Golden Eagle Protection Act and Migratory Bird Treaty Act.

Loraine and I took turns photographing one another leaning against the cottonwood. She said I was not the first to travel here from afar to have a photo taken beneath the eagle nest tree. She had greeted EagleCam watchers from California, Oregon and Idaho who wanted to see with their own eyes the nest and birds; some wanted to meet Loraine and Garry in person.

As I departed, Loraine said that if the tree and the nest were not a part of her life, she wouldn't be living there: "I feel that way about my tree. I feel that way about any tree. When I hear a chainsaw I just cringe. The natural part of our world is going away so fast and development is going up everywhere."

Loraine beside her eagle tree

According to the Washington Department of Natural Resources, between 1970 and 1995 the amount of land developed for homes and businesses doubled in the Puget Sound region. Despite the increase of human population on shorelines—the habitat of choice for eagles—eagles had increased too. In 1980, WDFW counted 105 nesting pairs. In 2005, they counted 856. By 2045, the number of people in Washington is expected to double to 11 million. Development that clears the land of big trees is a major threat to nesting eagles.

When Rick and Linda bought a piece of waterfront property over 20 years ago, unobstructed water views were popular. That view has not changed, nor has the preference of Rick and Linda. They prefer a "framed" view of Puget Sound.

The driveway that led me to their home in the summer of 2006 stopped at a two-storied home, where trees framed the water view. I parked beneath a basketball net and waited. A silver fir, perhaps 150 feet (45.7 m) tall, towered near the driveway. Beneath it were the signs of an online eagle nest within its branches: fallen sticks, eagle feathers and cable. Linda drove up and parked. We had arranged to meet and she invited me into her home. Once inside, I looked out through a window to see a big old Douglas-fir standing outside about 8 feet (2.4 m) from the house. "It has always bothered me to cut trees of this size," said Linda. "It's probably crazy on our part, but we angled the house around that tree to save it. We started with a very small house, and added a second story 18 years ago."

We climbed the stairs to the loft. Linda said they had to move the webcam TV upstairs to be able to focus on daily routines downstairs. Linda turned on the monitor. We watched, real-time, two baby eagles preening one another in the nest. Linda said the eaglets were about three and a half months old and about one and a half months shy of leaving the nest. I sat transfixed, watching the birds while Linda talked. She named their first pair of webcam eaglets in 2000. Linda's children, Molly and Mike, thought the names "Buff" and "Puff" were "froo-froo," but the names stuck for one more generation. After that, no one named the eaglets.

Mike bounded upstairs. He was 10 years old when their eagle tree went online. Today he was 16. He said watching eagles up close helped him see life from their perspective—what it's like to live with wind and storms that sway the canopy, how they learn to fly. At the moment on the webcam, an eaglet chewed on what appeared to be a bird. They were eating more birds this year, said Linda. Mike said his dad, Rick, had watched an eagle dive-bomb a heron in flight. Then Mike bounded downstairs and Molly bounded upstairs. Both Molly and Mike had summer jobs caring for small children.

Molly said she had been observing similarities between her family and successive generations of the same eagle pair: "You can see how dad treats them differently from how mom treats them. Dad feeds them very differently from how mom does. He'll tear bigger pieces off and if they don't want them, he'll eat the pieces himself. Mom makes sure she tears pieces small enough so they can eat them, which is very funny."

Molly was 18. She hadn't been watching the eaglets as much this year, she said. "But many times in the past when the eaglets were younger, if there were two of them, there would always be one who was smaller, either the male because females are bigger, or if they're both female or both male, it's the smaller one who doesn't get as much food. It's kind of the same thing in human relationships. One year there was only one of them. That was interesting too because mom prodded that one faster. Mom made that one get up and go faster. That one developed more independently than the others did."

I recalled what Chayce from Ocean Shores had said, that humans can learn a lot from eagles. They do show us how alike we are, and that we're a part of Nature too.

Molly said she sees how eagles need the trees and what kind of habitat they have to have. In 2005, the eagles moved 65 feet (19.8 m) away to an alternate nest on a neighbour's property. A year later Tim installed a camera in the new nest tree, and the line was spliced for both families to watch.

Molly continued: "When a big tree fell down in our driveway, it brought up whole new issues—what other trees are going to go, what trees do eagles have to have. It's really interesting for these eagles because, since the two of them have gotten so big, mom and dad don't sit in the nest anymore. In the evening you can look out of the window and they'll be in the bare tree, and the two of them will just perch there and have one eye on the nest and the other eye out on the water, fishing or whatever. It's really interesting. They just don't use one tree. They use multiple trees. They'll sit in top of the old nest tree and watch too. It's just their way of adapting to what's around them. If crows are being obnoxious one day, mom or dad will go and sit in the old nest and the crows will go there instead."

The eaglets are usually gone by the end of August, Molly said. "It's hard not to watch them take their first flight steps. They kind of throw themselves off the edge. Or mom forces them off the edge. I think it was two years ago, one of them took off. The other one wouldn't go for anything. Finally, mom just came up and herded him over the edge. He was being kinda wimpy. The other one had been gone for about two days."

Finally we tired of eagle watching on the webcam and descended from the loft. When Rick came home we watched a favourite of their many eagle videos: mom eagle tucking a mouthful of fish in baby's mouth, then turning her enormous beak to tidy baby's beak. "Now watch this," said Rick. Seconds after dad flew into the nest to drop a fish, an osprey flew up, talons first. Father eagle turned to lock talons midair, while mom puffed up, covering the eaglet with her tail. Rick replayed the video scene several times. It was fascinating and humbling to see how alike we are—how we both love, defend and protect our kind.

Rick recalled when Mike was shooting hoops nearby the nest. "All of a sudden this stick falls out of the tree. And I said, 'Mike, I think you're upsetting the eagles.' Mike just kind of laughed and did it again. And down comes another one. These were not little twigs. These were good sized sticks!"

"The funniest thing is when we have people over," said Linda, "and we say, 'Do you want to see the EagleCam?' 'Oh sure,' they say. 'Now where is this?' It's right out there, we say. 'What do you mean it's right out there?' So we have to go out and show the tree. And then there was this lady I was talking to about the birds, and she didn't believe me that there was an eagle nest right out in our backyard. We walked out the door as she was leaving, and just then one of the eagles flew out of the nest and a bunch of feathers came floating down."

I sensed the magic of that moment. It was more than beautiful feathers falling from the sky. It was acceptance of trees and eagles as part of the family—so uncommon in our society.

Rick said, "We've got two trees that are obviously dying and they're not nest trees, they're perch trees. People normally look at a dead tree and think it's a threat to their property. But I could not cut the tops out of those trees now because I know that the eagles might not find this a satisfactory place."

❦

Chapter Nine
ACCOUNTABILITY GROVES
Gifford Pinchot National Forest, Washington

As we walked into the 500-year-old research forest, Professor Jerry Franklin said, "These are my roots." He was a tall man with a long stride and I had to walk fast to keep up and take notes. I looked forward to the end of the path. We would lift off into the old growth canopy via North America's only canopy crane.

In 1995 Jerry brought the crane to the Munger Research Natural Area (the RNA), which is inside the Wind River Experimental Forest, which is inside the Gifford Pinchot National Forest in southern Washington. The RNA had long been called the "Cradle of Forest Research in the Pacific Northwest," and Jerry had long been called the "Guru of Old-Growth." Like the trees, Jerry was indigenous to this place. His middle name is Forest. He grew up in Camas, about 35 miles (56 km) west of the forest. By the time he was eight years old, he and his family camped among the forest's old-growth. By the time he was ten, he wanted to be a forester. At 16 he rode his family's Model T Ford into the Munger RNA, and thought the RNA was a good idea. In the 1960s while a research forester, he had a hunch that there was more to a Douglas-fir old growth forest than board feet. While directing the Andrews Ecosystem Research Project, Jerry realized that the forest canopy was important to the forest and decided they needed better tools. Congress delivered funds to buy a crane that had once installed a library in San Francisco. The crane plus installation cost US$1.2 million.

Along the path to the crane stood a sign. It read:

Scientists reach new heights in canopy exploration. Imagine climbing a 200-foot (60.9-m) tree with no branches for the first 100 feet (30.5 m) and with the top branches and tips too fragile to support your weight. Now scientists need not fret about reaching these heights. The crane allows them to stretch their arms and imaginations to the tops of the trees for a better understanding of forest health. . . .

For researchers from the University of Washington or Pacific Northwest Research Station, crane trips were free. For most others, trips cost $182 an hour. I was neither researcher nor most others. My husband Richard was a friend and colleague of Jerry, who had invited mostly Richard for a tour of the facility in September 2004. While they talked about forest regeneration, I looked around.

The collapse of Douglas-firs along the path revealed infection by velvet top fungus, I was told. Jerry said the fungus felled half the Douglas-firs in this forest, and the Douglas-fir was giving up its dominance. It is thought that a fire torched this landscape about 500 years ago. When the forest grew back, Douglas-firs grew above the others, not liking shade. Then trees like western hemlock and western redcedar filled up the lower canopy. Douglas-firs were the giants here, explained Jerry, but they were not reproducing because their seedlings couldn't get a start in the shade.

We reached a bulletin board that warned: "Overhead hazards. Research in progress." A map showed the position of every standing tree, living or dead, within the crane's reach. I looked beyond the path and saw a grey boardwalk leading into the forest. White tubes protruded from the floor and grey boxes rose up on metal pipes, to which power cords attached, weaving snake-like above and below ground from a small hut beneath the crane. Every fallen branch was tagged, and most likely counted.

We walked toward the crane and looked up. It was a box-like frame of metal with a ladder inside, perfectly vertical for 75 metres (250 ft). I had to bend my neck to see its top, and follow the jib, a horizontal metal arm of 85 metres (278.8 ft). To keep it standing, the crane was bolted to a 635,000-kg (635-ton) concrete block beneath the forest floor.

The crane operator began to climb the ladder rungs to the top of the crane, where he would manipulate the giant machine from within a cabin above. Then an arbonaut stepped forward from a small outbuilding. Giving us harnesses to put on, he said that in case of power failure, we would need to climb down. I trusted that would not be necessary.

We stepped into the yellow gondola on the ground. The jib held it from above like a pendulum. By rope and hook we attached ourselves to a side of the gondola. The arbonaut Ken Bible entered. As gondola operator, Ken would communicate by radio with the crane operator. Ken asked me if I was afraid of heights. If I vomit, I said, I will lean over the side and you will know. As we lifted off I was surprised to feel little vertical motion.

Ten, twenty, fifty feet and rising. I kept a steady gaze on the forest floor. Vine maple leaves below us glowed neon green and yellow in the sunlight. Water puddles on the forest floor reflected sky and clouds above.

Being inside the canopy of an old-growth forest, you can see how it's "bottom loaded," Jerry pointed out. What I saw was the foliage of old trees bulging at ground level like Victorian era petticoats. Jerry said, "We knew these trees had deep canopies, but they shouldn't have, because they pruned themselves when they were young." When the forest was young, he explained, it was top heavy with live branches. As the forest matured, the canopy inverted. "We knew that, but we really didn't know it, in a sense. We'd seen data that said that, but it wasn't really until we got into the stand and did the work to see that the canopies are not just rough—they're continuous with foliage from the ground to the top."

At 100 feet (30.5 m) and rising, we passed the top of a snag. The crane allowed researchers to observe snags safely; climbing their decayed limbs was risky. Then we slid horizontally along the jib to enter the canopy of a grand fir. Rising higher in the gaps of canopy, we passed clouds of needle flumes. When we rose above the shorter trees, I startled at the broad view of tree tops, sensing this would be an opportunity-of-a-lifetime experience.

Ken pointed to the "sun foliage"—the needles on the treetops. They were smaller, thicker, more erect—features that more than one canopy researcher was observing. Ken said the dominant theory was that needle shape is controlled by water pressure. "We used the crane to go slowly up the crown and take pressure readings right here in the gondola to get an idea of the changes in pressure values from the morning when everything is in equilibrium with soil moisture, all the way into the afternoon when the extreme vapour pressure deficit is going on. The higher you go, the harder it is to get that water up there."

As we neared the top level of this expensive fresh-air elevator, I beheld the Cascade Range running north and south, with multiple ridges spanning east to west. The vastness of the view filled me with awe. Jerry distracted me: "One of the other aspects of the canopy," he said, "besides its continuous nature and the fact that it's bottom loaded, is how rugose, how very rugged the canopy topography is. What you notice here at the top is no continuous canopy in the way of a young forest. Instead, the canopy is a series of peaks and valleys." He said one of the canopy researchers was studying the rumple factor of the rugosity.

Number 91
and canopy
crane

"We're coming up on tree Number 91," said Ken as the gondola and jib sliced a piece of invisible pie in the sky. "This is the tallest one that the crane can access. It's about 65 metres (213.25 ft) to the top."

"Tree Number 91? Doesn't it have a name?" I asked. Of all the big trees I had met, most had names given by their caretakers. Ken said he thought an RNA researcher named Roaki called it Goliath. Jerry did not respond. He asked Ken if this was the tree they were using for the irrigation experiment. Ken said yes, it's the one where they provided water through an IV to small branches in the tree top to see if Douglas-firs absorb water through their twig bark. They knew that redwoods take in moisture through their branches, but they didn't know if Douglas-firs do.

As we gazed upon the treetops, Ken said Number 91 was not the biggest tree within the RNA. Pointing to a tree outside the crane's reach—a circular plot of 2.3 hectares (6 acres)—he said, "One of the tallest is this guy right out here. It's about 70 metres (229.7 ft) high. That's about it for this particular site. The water seems to be a big factor in limiting height growth."

The jib lowered to look at hemlock infected with dwarf mistletoe. I could see patches of the stuff nesting here and there. The Douglas-fir and western redcedar were not infected. "It makes a good case for the whole notion of mixed stands and spatial heterogeneity in your composition," said Jerry.

As the gondola slid along the jib, and the jib swirled to a tree poking above the lower strata of needle clouds, Jerry explained canopy zones. There are three—dim, transition and bright, he said. "I had thought the bright zone was hot and dry and nothing would be going on here. It turns out that it's a real hot spot for biodiversity. The silver spotted tiger moth is a really great example of a species that's an upper canopy specialist. It's a winter-active caterpillar that develops colonies on the south side of the tallest Douglas-fir canopy, at the very top. That's just a special example. Basically there's a tremendous amount of diversity and activity here."

"Let's go look at the CO_2 sensors," said Jerry.

Ken spoke to the crane operator: "Mark, we'd like to go ahead now to the CO_2 station please."

The gondola slid along the jib to stop near the tower. I could see a sensor attached near the top of the crane. Ken pointed to a rectangle of wire tubing attached to the side of the tower. He said it measured wind speed in three directions, ten times a second. Another tube sucked in air ten times a second to measure moisture and CO_2. A big black box on the crane digitized the information by an infrared gas analyzer, and sent numbers to computers in the research centre for counting.

Time was up, said Ken. Down below, summer work students were waiting for a canopy ride. Vertical descent through the upper canopy revealed swirls of spiral branches full of cones. Gaps of space among dense foliage defined the transition zone. Jerry said the spotted owls need both space and density. "In fact, when we first started getting up here, I argued that one of the most important aspects of the canopy is the voids. Well I was righter than I thought!"

Reaching the ground we removed our harnesses and followed a boardwalk into the forest plot beneath the crane. Jerry said you can watch a bubble of CO_2 enriched air move up through the forest at night. It hangs right at the top until the sun comes in the morning, and then it pops.

"Can you see the bubble?" I asked.

"You see it in the data," he said.

I blushed over my literal interpretation. We passed by the huge mound surrounding the base of Number 91, and I dared to ask the same question again—why wasn't the tallest tree referred to by name? Naming was so common in tree culture.

"People here just haven't adopted names for trees," replied Jerry, slightly irritated. "They deal with too many trees. I think probably our crane operator would have a little bit of trouble with that. He's got an XYZ coordinator and he knows every one of the trees by number."

I met Roaki at the Tenth Annual Wind River Canopy Crane Research Conference in 2004. Actually his name was Hiroaki Ishii, but he said people in North America called him Roaki so they didn't have to say "hi" twice. He gave a talk at the conference about his research, about how the

Douglas-fir reestablishes its crown at maturity and maintains its old age. He had started his research as a graduate student on a Fulbright scholarship at the University of Washington, where Professor Jerry Franklin taught about the forest ecosystem.

At the conference I asked Roaki if I could tag along during his research at the Munger RNA. He said the next time would depend on funding and that he lived in Japan.

In the meantime, we emailed. I asked if it was he who named Number 91 Goliath. He said he had not. But he did name all the trees he climbed for his PhD research. He explained: "It is fitting that one names trees that one climbs, as one's life depends on the tree (literally hangs on it)." Ishi was the first tree he climbed, named after himself. Then came five Douglas-firs nearby—Talperian, Windy, Pan, Papa Bear, and Locs Next. He preferred to climb for research, although he had started in the Wind River Canopy Crane.

Roaki said he would like to take me up into one of his Douglas-firs that he studied for his PhD. What climbing gear and experience did I have, he asked. I replied that I had one experience with a trained guide and a lot of safety gear, and another experience with a treesitter and no gear. All I could do on the "free climb" without gear was to put my foot in the rope loop and dangle side to side. With safety gear and a lot of coaching, I was slow to ascend, I said, but was keen to try again.

In October 2006 I arrived at the Wind River Experimental Forest. Roaki invited me to stay with his team at the Forest Service bunkhouse. This would be his eighth field season.

For the next morning, the plan was to rise before dawn to meet Roaki in the forest. But I continued to sleep instead. While I slept, Roaki drove to the RNA and parked near the chain link fence that bordered it. Behind the fence stood a cross section of an old-growth forest—tall and short trees and snags in every stage of decomposition. Roaki passed through the gate, followed an old logging road, turned onto a path carved over logs, stepping on a network of moss-covered roots rising from the floor like veins surfacing under the skin of old hands. The path twisted around trees and below branches with drooping lichen. He stopped before the biggest Douglas-fir in his study plot that Roaki had named after himself. About 500 years ago, after the last fire swept through the forest, Ishi had sprouted.

Near the foot of Ishi lay a blue tarp that covered Roaki's equipment. Roaki poked beneath the tarp, found climbing gear and put it on. He clipped a bag of water to his harness. The bag would contain a stem from the very top of Ishi. Roaki had a hypothesis to prove. He wanted to advance the theory about the physiological processes that define the maximum height that a Douglas-fir could achieve. Because of the difficulty in getting water all the way to the treetop, the needles at the top of really tall Douglas-firs—sun foliage—are smaller than those lower down. Roaki proposed that it's the small needle size that limits height growth. Smaller needles capture less sunlight for photosynthesis than regular needles.

Roaki untied the rope from Ishi's base. The 120-metre-long (393.7-ft) rope ran through a pulley that was tied to a belt, which was wrapped around the upper trunk. One end of the rope dangled from the upper canopy. The other end was tied to the base of the tree. Roaki stood back from Ishi and looked up. The tree stood 65 metres (213.25 ft) tall, while Roaki measured much less. He had composed a haiku about it:

Perched at the tree top
I sway in southerly wind
Feel how small am I

With carabiners clanging and stirrups dangling from his body, Roaki bent forward before Ishi with one long bow. Then he climbed.

Roaki's ascent

It was the reasonable hour of 8:30 a.m. when I entered the research area. Roaki had expected me much earlier. Luckily I found him on the ground. I apologized and explained that dinner of the previous night had disagreed with me. Weakened and fatigued, I felt ill-prepared for a tree climb, but was willing nonetheless. I had interrupted Roaki's schedule, but he patiently showed me how to put on the climbing gear. I donned a padded harness for the waist with pads for the underside of each thigh. Everything attached to an umbilical carabiner, including the ascenders, which were clamps on the rope. Roaki put on his gear and demonstrated how to use it on the rope. He raised the bottom ascender to his chest, which raised his feet in the stirrups. Standing in the stirrups, he slid the top ascender upward. To descend, he wove the rope into an upside-down metal U with horizontal clasps, detached ascenders, and slipped down.

Then I tried. I got my feet into the stirrups OK, but the rope was so elastic I bounced and bumped into the trunk. Sliding one ascender on the rope, I stood up and repeated. After climbing several feet above ground, I wanted to make sure I could descend. I fumbled with the metal U, gave up on it, and used the ascenders in reverse to go down. Roaki had better things to do than watch my wavering efforts, and left me on my own to practice. As I slowly slid up and down, I listened to words in Japanese gaily shouted through the canopy. Two climbers from Roaki's team were tagging branches in the canopy.

Roaki left the study area with his tree-top stems, heading for the Canopy Hut—the RNA research centre. Near the fence on his way out, he plucked a stem from the top of a short Douglas-fir using a pole saw. The needles of that stem were regular in size. Then he climbed the fence to take a fish-eye photo of the sky seen from the treetop. The photo would document the light available as the sun passed overhead. The tops of Ishi and the short tree had the same azimuth. Roaki continued onward to the research centre.

At the lab, Roaki put the Douglas-fir stems in tubes of water to keep them hydrated. He placed one set of stems outside the building and the other set inside, in a dark room. He would use them to compare the photosynthetic and water-holding capacity of needles from tall and short trees.

In the meantime, I came down from my ascent of a few feet and walked through an open field to the research centre. I found Roaki in the lab, using a "pressure bomb," a small concentric chamber to measure hydraulic pressure in the stems. Roaki darted outside to collect the stems in test tubes. Returning to the lab, he plucked the stems into smaller units. One by one, he set them inside a small, clear chamber that measured the rate of CO_2 the stems absorbed. Roaki rotated the stems

Sun foliage from Ishi (right) and young Douglas-fir (left)

under artificial light. He wanted to imitate the angles that sunlight would have struck them outside. He photographed each stem upon a light table. Finally, he plucked apart the stems to count the needle surface area.

"That looks really tedious," I remarked.

Roaki looked up from keyboarding, breaking his concentration. "Yes," he said. "It's tedious until the numbers come in, and then it's exciting." He took another break to smile.

On the next day of Roaki's research, I aspired to reach the upper limits of Ishi. I had learned that to climb up, it was best not to look down. So I repeated the actions of ascent like a mantra. Raise the bottom ascender to the chest; pull up the stirrups. Raise the top ascender; stand up. Repeat. After numerous repetitions, I took a break. With nothing else to do, I stared at Ishi. For a 500-year-old tree, he was tall but not too thick. I knew his top peaked above all the trees in the study plot and I wanted to get to that top. I looked at Ishi's strong trunk and recommitted to ascend. But then I paused to visualize the insides of my support, that I ascended with the water that Ishi's plumbing lifted to every needle. Deep inside the trunk the xylem lifted both water and minerals from the roots. The cambium was growing wood cells to give the tree its girth. Beneath the bark was the phloem, a pipe for nutrients from the photosynthesis in needles flowing downward. Even the needles had pipes, and the needle surface had stomata to breathe in carbon dioxide and transpire oxygen and water vapour. For this alone I sensed how much I depended on this tree and all others. I breathed in the oxygen it gave me and exhaled gratitude.

Just then my rope dropped two inches. My heart bounced. My hands gripped the ascenders and I held on tight. The carabiner attached to my harness had rotated. I sat suspended in my padded seat. If I leaned back, the harness would dig into my rib cage. Above me Roaki dangled on another rope, plucking stems, taking photographs, and likely enjoying the scenic view. I wanted to reach him, but I could see him coming down. When our eyes met, I looked around and realized that I had only reached the first living branch of Ishi.

"So this is the first branch?" I asked.

"Yes," said Roaki, "this is the lowest branch on the tree, which is about 25 metres (82 ft) above ground." Roaki smiled. "Good job," he said. "This is actually an epicormic branch. It's probably less than 100 years old. You can see how thin it is."

It looked more like a short stick with green bristles. An aluminum tag hung from it, being tied on with a green twist tie. Number 149 identified the tag. All the branches of this tree were tagged and numbered. All the branches of the other Douglas-firs in the study plot—all 2000 of them— had been tagged and counted too. They were measured for length, thickness and height from ground. Roaki said branch number 149 was a branch regenerating.

"Why would it regenerate?" My voice quivered. I was becoming apprehensive from hanging on a rope for life support. Even though its breaking strength was 3000 kg (3 tons), it was still a rope.

"As the forest was developing, it got dark and many of the lower branches died," he explained. "But then as the forest matured and began to age, trees began to die around Ishi. Look, there's two broken snags on each side of this tree."

I peeked at the trees around us. Gaps in the canopy created by dead trees let in rays of sunlight. My eyes returned to branch number 149.

"What's the big deal about epicormic branching?" I asked.

"Well, it would have been nice to show you!" Roaki replied. If we go higher, you can see a branch about 20 centimetres (7.8 in) thick. About 10 centimetres (3.9 in) from the base it forks into five different directions, and each branch is 5 centimetres (1.9 in) thick. It's like a platform that you can sit on. That occurs through epicormic branching. The tip of the original branch is broken, but proximal to where it broke, a bunch of sprouts came out from dormant buds beneath the bark. They all grew and spread out in different directions. It almost looks like a hand spreading out from the trunk."

It was Roaki who discovered the significance of epicormic branching to the long life of Douglas-firs. When Douglas-firs reach their maximum height, he proved they stay alive by resprouting foliage from established branches. Above us about 10 metres (32.8 ft) higher extended more branches that could resprout.

Roaki said, "You know how people like to gather logs on the beach because they look gnarly and interesting? A lot of dead branches in Ishi have that character too."

I looked up. "Yeah, it looks pretty gnarly up there. But there's not a lot of thick branches you can sit on." As though I would venture to do that. I looked at Roaki. He was smiling. "You look pretty comfortable," I remarked.

"Yeah, it's nice up here," he said.

I looked at Ishi and then at Roaki. "I don't see any similarity between you two besides the name."

"No, I'm not exactly the tallest person. Maybe the way the tree leans."

I dared to push myself away from the trunk with my foot in the stirrup. "Yeah, it is leaning," I said.

"It's like it's bowing to the sun," said Roaki. "It leans to the southeast, and bows to where the sun comes up from. So me being from the Far East, and the country of the rising sun, I think of it as showing respect to the sun, a source of energy and source of photosynthesis for life. In that sense I feel a fondness for it. I've spent a lot of time in this tree thinking about different things. I went to an exhibit in Seattle of Chinese thinking stones. The stones had gnarly patterns that Chinese philosophers used to collect and put on their desks because they provoked thought. The patterns on the dead branches and the bark of Ishi, when I look at them up close, I see a similarity. I see patterns that provoke thought. Yeah, I've spent a lot of time hanging around this tree."

"Does the tree give you perspective?"

"It gives me an appreciation. These branches beneath you on the hemlock, they're so beautiful in design. The foliage looks like intricate lace work that's laid out perfectly and beautifully to capture the light that's coming from above. You don't get this perspective just standing on the ground. When you come up close to the bole, you see all this death and birth going on with branches. It provokes me to think about how trees rotate and regenerate their branches. The longevity of Douglas-firs is 1200 years or so, and they last, most of them, about 600 to 800 years in the forest. When I think about that, I wonder how they do that. I think this constant regenerating process of epicormic branching is part of that."

Roaki kept smiling as he hung on the rope. He said sometimes he worked in the canopy for six hours at a time, ate lunch on the rope, and used a pee bottle. If it got windy, he might rock back and forth a metre (3.3 ft) each way. "That does feel weird," he admitted. "When you get down it feels like getting off a ship and you're still rocking."

Another reason canopy research was not my calling. I am prone to seasickness.

"There's many aspects about trees," he continued. "You realize how beautifully and perfectly they are designed. Just growing cones at the top is part of that design. The higher up they are, the farther the seeds can fly."

"So that's a reproductive means of Douglas-fir?" I asked. "The taller it gets, the more it can spread its seeds?"

"Yeah, you can see in the branches right above us there are no cones. The tree knows where to put its cones."

"Where did you take your branch today for the measurements?" I asked.

"About a fifth branch level down from the top, a little bit further in the southeast," said Roaki.

"I noticed that the higher I climbed it seemed easier to pull my weight up," I said.

"Yeah, you get less stretch of the rope as you go up higher so you're not bouncing around as much. Also, the weight of the rope beneath you allows you to pull up the lower ascender without having to hold the rope down."

I considered going up. But with Roaki going down, I would be on my own. "OK, I'm ready to go down now," I said.

I wove the rope in and out of the metal U. Roaki checked my weave and I removed the ascenders. We descended together. When I took off my gear, I was shaking. Roaki empathized. He said it took him half of a field season to overcome his fear of climbing. "At first I thought it was primitive and dangerous. So I put in two ropes and attached myself to both. Gradually I got used to one rope." Roaki was as polite to humans as to trees.

At the end of the last day of research, he said, his team will collect at the forest gate. They will line up to face the forest and bow. It's the way to show respect for what supports you.

North of the RNA in the Gifford Pinchot National Forest is a place called Government Mineral Springs. Jerry Franklin's parents hiked there on their first date, and Jerry and his wife got married there, in a grove of old-growth. For the past 25 years, Jerry has used the grove to contemplate. "To sit in the context of a forest environment," he explained to me, "provides you with a much more thoughtful context than just sitting in a room somewhere. It makes you more aware of what values are involved and what your professed motivation is. It helps to take it out of the personal and put it more in the context of the world ecosystem."

Jerry took me to see the small grove. The circle of trees allowed a person to stand within it, look upward at the mix of deciduous leaves and evergreen needles, and feel centred. Jerry stepped inside the circle and then I did. I imagined the invisible budding of epicormic branches, the amazing feat of hydraulic lift into every needle of sun foliage, and the expiration of oxygen that enable me to breathe. I said the place was awesome.

Jerry looked up. "But there has to be more than awe," he said. "There's got to be incredible value beyond esthetics, and there is."

I sensed a profound appreciation for the complexity of the forest, and that Nature must reveal herself to those who immerse themselves within her.

Jerry Franklin
in his grove

ॐ

Chapter Ten
MEGAMORPHOSIS
Ashland, Oregon

I had been living in Ashland, Oregon for several years when the *New York Times* reported it to be among the country's most livable cities with populations of 20,000. Ashland was also renowned for its Oregon Shakespeare Theater and Lithia Park, thanks to the foresight of the Women's Civic Improvement Club. In 1908 the women spearheaded the creation of Lithia Park, and promoted proper landscaping everywhere. Perhaps the first environmental activists of Ashland, they also raised money for a few small parks and a piece of land to save an endangered tree. It appeared that their values survived them. Since 1985, Ashland had been recognized as a Tree City USA, adorned by 240 different tree species.

It was a Saturday in November 2000 when I walked downtown to the library. Approaching from the sidewalk, I noticed a sign at the foot of a large Deodora cedar that stood beside the front stairs of the library. In handwritten letters, the sign announced "Day Two." I looked up into the tree's canopy to discover a cable connecting the cedar to a large ginkgo tree standing further east of the building on library grounds. Tracing the cable back to the cedar, I spied a platform perched in the upper branches. From the platform hung a white bucket that was sitting on the ground. I looked inside to find a walkie talkie, which I picked it up.

"What are you protesting?" I asked.

"I voted for the library expansion without knowing that they were gonna tear out that ginkgo tree and 26 other trees and plants, big bushes," said a male voice. "In 1994, the *Mail Tribune* came by, and asked me to bring my dogs inside so they could take a picture of my dogs in the library, because there was a group of people that didn't want dogs and pets in the library. And those people were successful in their endeavours. And now pets can't go in there. We can't even leave our pets out in front of the library anymore. And now they want to kill the park. That isn't the essence of Ashland. That's not the personality of the community that I knew when I was attracted here."

"So you have strong feelings for the ginkgo?" I asked.

"First of all, the tree is special. I used to sit under it all the time. Yes, the tree is special to me, the whole park is special to me. The whole park." The small park he referred to graced the side and front entrance of the library.

"How long do you plan on sitting up there?" I asked.

"Until the whole matter is resolved," he said.

I put the walkie talkie back in the bucket. A woman approached from the coffee shop across the street, carrying hot coffee and a sandwich. She placed the items in the bucket, which the treesitter pulled up to the platform. The treesit had local support.

I noticed a woman in her 40s and man in his 30s talking near the ginkgo at the other end of the library park. As I approached them, I heard the woman talking about how ginkgoes and Dawn redwoods are the oldest living trees on the planet.

"And that's not something to just chop down," she continued. "We need to honour that and we need to build around it. Maybe the fact that we can respect something like this tree is more important than a lot of books you can check out from the library. The process that you go through to honour what we have here, this treasure—you can't get that from books."

The man said, "Maybe in the 1850s and 1860s when the settlers came to this area, if they had respect for the trees, they wouldn't have barbarically massacred the local Native Americans. Respect could actually grow for different species."

"But don't you think the library needs to be expanded?" I interjected. "It does need more space for books and such." I was a frequent library user.

"Yeah, but not $750,000 over budget," replied the woman. "It doesn't need to be expanded that much. We need to work within our budget. And we need to work with our ginkgo tree."

"What makes you want to save the ginkgo?" I asked, unconvinced. The tree was mature, but it wasn't a towering old growth, and many other mature trees populated Ashland.

"The fact that it's so beautiful. It's lost a lot of its leaves right now, but they're like flakes of gold. The wind blows and they're fluttering to the ground. It's just awe-inspiring. Just the fact that there it is, beautiful in all seasons. When you come in early spring, and these little tiny leaf buds are coming out, they're brilliant rich green. And then it's fall—the leaves are more beautiful than gold. And there's piles of leaves. I scoop them up and bring them home and put them in bowls. I paint them, the little tiny details, in watercolour paintings. And the fact that it's an historical tree to this city. The daughter of an original settler planted it here, and the fact that it's a living fossil, one of the oldest trees on this planet. The combination of it all, I can't fathom anyone walking around this site and drawing up a plan that's going to destroy it. What kind of an architect could do that? What kind of a city council could pass that? And I think a lot of people who voted for it didn't know what they were voting for."

"That's true," I admitted, recollecting. "I didn't know I was voting to cut down the trees." Had I gone to see the design of the expansion at the library, I would have noticed that this treed park was missing from the picture. On the other hand, the ballots of two elections did not ask voters to approve the felling of a tree with historical value.

She continued: "The city council is saying, 'Well, this is what the voters wanted.' And we said, 'No, we didn't know what you were going to do. And OK, maybe we were naïve, maybe we were dumb. You know what? We found out a big mistake was made. Let's please fix it. Let's not destroy something and have to live with that mistake forever.'"

"So you're supporting the treesit?" I asked.

"Oh yeah, absolutely. I come here a couple times a day. I bought him the walkie talkies."

I smiled and parted company. Entering the library, I pondered how the ginkgo meant so much to her. She treated the golden leaves like they really did contain flakes of gold.

Eleven days later I read about the treesitter in the local newspaper. Rick Harris was listening to music on his portable CD player, preparing to go to sleep in his canopy tent. He felt vibrations from the platform and then it gave way. Branches twisted the tent and Rick hung upside down. He yelled for help and someone called the police. Fortunately, the rescue crew arrived in 22 seconds because the fire station stood across the street. A firefighter scrambled up a ladder and pulled Rick from the tent, accidentally pulling off his thermal underwear at the same time. Naked in the spotlight with a crowd gawking on the ground, Rick put on his pants and climbed down with help. He was afraid of heights.

While waiting for the platform to be repaired, Rick enjoyed a Thanksgiving meal on the ground. Then he climbed back into the canopy. Feeling the platform to be unstable, he came down. Still committed to the cause, he volunteered to be a lookout for the next treesitter, but no one took up the post.

A week or so later, poking around the Ashland Public Library, I discovered bits of history providing context to the controversy.

The library park had once been the backyard of Mrs. Otto Winter. She planted the ginkgo about 1900, and it was now the oldest ginkgo bilboa in Southern Oregon. Mrs. Winter was also one of the founders of the Women's Civic Improvement Club—a fact suitable for nominating the tree for heritage tree status, had there been a heritage tree program in Ashland.

The ginkgo species is native to Asia and considered a living fossil, being about 250 million years old. About seven million years ago it was also native to the Pacific Northwest, where its remains were discovered at the site of what is now the Petrified Ginkgo Forest in southern Washington. It's a hardy tree and revered for its persistence. The male of the species excels on city streets, resisting disease and pollutants, fire, and even atomic bombs. The ginkgo that stood beside a Hiroshima temple survived the World War II atomic blast by resprouting. When consideration was given to cutting down the tree to rebuild the temple, the final choice was to build around the tree. Likewise in Salem, Oregon Governor Mark Hatfield protected a ginkgo near the Labor and Industry

Ginkgo
beside the
library
parking lot

building. He insisted its construction not risk the tree's life, at least for one year after completion, when he approved final payment to the building contractor.

A different fate for the Ashland Library ginkgo had been sealed by a November 1999 vote to remodel and expand the Carnegie library on its existing site. Six months later, a county-wide election approved a bond to upgrade all the county libraries to serve increased populations. Unlike Ashland, the nearby City of Medford decided that its Carnegie building would become an historic and cultural landmark within its park setting; a new Medford Library with convenient parking would be built downtown. Carnegie libraries were legacies of the wealthy US industrialist Andrew Carnegie, who began to fund libraries throughout the world in the late 19th century. In the post-Civil War era, women's clubs emerged to promote culture generally, and often spearheaded the establishment of libraries.

I asked Ashland librarian Bob Wilson about the decision to remodel the 1909 Carnegie Ashland Library on its existing site, instead of relocating it. "The problem was," he explained, "if we vacated the Carnegie, what was going to happen to it? It might have lasted another five or six years. It leaked everywhere—the walls, the roof, and the basement." The city owned the Carnegie property, the Carnegie needed restoration, and another site would cost more money.

"The irony of the whole thing," the librarian asserted, "was that the ginkgo was dying because they had put in a parking lot in 1972. It would have been completely dead in another 15, 20 years."

I asked the city's horticulturalist about the health of the tree. Don Todt disagreed with the librarian: "When you cover the ground with asphalt, tree roots don't get as much air or water. But there is subsurface water on that site, so the tree was probably getting enough water. The tree was healthy." Responding to the claim that when the parking lot was paved, dirt was piled around the ginkgo, causing it to rot, Don said there was nothing in the foliage showing the tree was in decline. "Ultimately the large limb that was removed to put in the parking lot would have affected the tree's longevity. But do we need to take out a tree because it's dying, like the rest of us, from old age?"

On another afternoon in November, I walked by the library park and noticed a man with long gray hair sitting beside the ginkgo on a bench. A big bag of popcorn, perhaps collected for bird feeding, sat at his feet. A few people had gathered nearby and I stopped to join them. The man removed a small notepad from his pocket and read outloud from it:

Tree People

Shall the <u>hu</u> mans kill all of us?
Progress
is the word concept
of a people obsessed with growth and the fire of their desires.
Anything in their way is subject to death or removal.
This time it's the Tree People.
They speak but the <u>hu</u> man only hears his own personal heart.
Will you
break away
from the pack of ever expanding <u>hu</u> man ideas?
Now is the time.
Do we watch old life destroyed and then displayed as books?
A tree is more glorious, absolutely divine,
and perfectly contented.
Let them Live.

While listening to the recitation, I noted the poet's emphasis on "hu." To me, that hinted of hubris—wanton insolence and arrogance. Could we really hear the Tree People speak, I wondered. Maybe we could, if we chose to be humble enough to listen. But then, how do you listen to a tree?

Colin Swales was a design/builder who specialized in historic preservation. He owned an 1884 historic home across the alley from the library. I went to visit him, to learn more about his concerns for the ginkgo. Earlier in the same year, Colin had started a campaign to nominate it as Ashland Tree of the Year. Another feature of the tree to merit its preservation: not only was it the oldest ginkgo bilboa in Southern Oregon; it was also the only large female ginkgo in Southern Oregon.

We sat inside Colin's living room, tastefully decorated with respect for heritage. He told me about contacting a woman in the Netherlands, Cor Kwant, who operated a website about ginkgo trees. He said she gained a lot of support to save the Ashland ginkgo from her world-wide audience, basically, people who are interested in ginkgo trees. Cor even wrote letters to Ashland City Council to save the tree.

Unknown to Colin, Cor had also offered his collection of Ashland Library ginkgo seeds on an international seed-swapping website. Colin said people from across the US and Europe contacted him to obtain Ashland Library ginkgo seeds. Being one of the oldest species on the planet, the ginkgo knew how to survive.

On January 2, 2001, another activist climbed the ginkgo to hang tissue-paper butterflies in its barren branches. Among a small group looking on stood newly-elected mayor Alan DeBoer. He had expressed reservations about the library expansion a month before taking office. The lowest bid for construction was three-quarters of a million dollars over budget and parking was inadequate. Even the mayor-elect joined the plea to send the project back for redesign.

That same month, the construction job went out for rebidding instead of redesign. Jackson County lawyers had advised that changing the library site or its design, as approved by the voters, could lead to litigation, and worse—personal liability for the city councillors. Four months later, a local contractor won the contract—still $177,000 over budget. Construction would begin soon, expanding a 7000-square foot (650.3-m²) building with 16 parking spaces to 23,000 square feet (2136.8 m²), with 13 parking spaces, even though the people had also voted for more parking.

With the ginkgo clearly doomed, Colin did more research. He discovered that ginkgoes can resprout from their root ball, and hoped to save the tree by soaking the stump. Others were expecting 24-hour notice before the library trees were cut down.

Around 6 a.m. on June 26, 2001, Colin answered a call from a neighbour who said loggers were assembling at the library. Colin rushed out and crossed the alley to the park. On the way, he heard the crack of wood. He called newly-elected city councillor Cate Hartzell. His voice was shaking like there had been an earthquake. She got dressed and rushed over to the library. She found the mayor, Colin and the head librarian there. She heard the mayor apologizing, like: This is the way I decided to do it because we were worried about protestors.

When the rest of the town woke up, if they passed by the library, they would have discovered the ginkgo on the ground. Two outraged brothers saw fit to lodge themselves in the shrubs and small trees while the logging continued. What the mayor feared had come to pass, but in a new form—bush-sitting. One gave up easily to police custody, while it took four police to dislodge the other. Both were banned from the library.

While the banning of the brothers would be lifted later, championed by the mayor himself and public outcry, another outrage continued, frequently voiced in the public forum of the *Ashland Daily Tidings*. Some had hoped to be present for the tree felling, to be witness and to mourn. Referring to "the massacre at our town library," resident Alan Sasha Lithman wrote in the newspaper: "Perhaps for some, it was only trees. For me, it was a great deal more that got cut down: Trust, transparency, mutual respect, diversity, inclusiveness, collaboration, a willingness to work through conflict toward deeper resolution of core values. In other words, the very roots that support and nurture community and a more conscious practice of democracy."

I was beginning to value the ginkgo beyond it being a tree. And I felt betrayed as well. It was a tree cherished by many, and because of that, I cherished it through the hearts of others.

About a week after the ginkgo was felled, a local wood sculptor went to the library to see if he could get some free wood from the logged library trees. The construction manager on site said they were going to haul it all away, but the sculptor could speak to the mayor to get some wood. Not inclined to get involved in "politics," the sculptor decided to ask for the ginkgo stump; he had been told they were going to dump it in a landfill. A few days later, he returned to the library. While waiting for the stump to be excavated, he talked with library staff. They told him they were glad the ginkgo was gone because the fruit smelled like dog shit and made a mess on people and their cars.

As the sculptor drove away with the 1000-lb (453.6-kg) ginkgo stump in his truck, Colin discovered what was happening. He ran after the truck, taking pictures of the license plate. The construction company had not been informed that Colin planned to resprout the stump.

City councillor Cate Hartzell contacted the sculptor and went to talk to him. But the stump had started to dry, so she left with pieces of root. She didn't recall any decision at city council about what could be done with the library trees, so she tracked down the logs. She sat on the logger's porch until he came home. He said if it was such a big deal, they could buy back the logs.

The mayor bought the logs. Cate arranged for their milling and the mayor paid for it. The timber went to dry on the car sales lot of the mayor's Chevrolet business. Of the ginkgo wood alone, there were about 500 board feet. Cate thought that one way to heal the community was to involve it in transforming the wood. She hoped that some of the wood would go to the wood shop of the local high school. The library wanted a podium, a table, a bookcase, and perhaps a bench for the library park—what was left of it.

Being one of the oldest species on the planet, the ginkgo knew how to survive.

In June 2002, the City of Ashland adopted a tree ordinance after extensive public comment. It recognized heritage trees and provided some protection for trees on development and city-owned property: such trees "have the potential to affect significantly larger numbers of persons if unregulated."

Eight months later, the sculptor began to carve the ginkgo stump. He discovered that a third of the stump was rotten, and declared to local media that the tree had been dying. Two weeks before the new library's grand opening in May 2003, he completed the sculpture. The Friends of the Library bought it and placed it in the children's department. The ginkgo stump was transformed into two pieces—an open book imprinted with the shape of butterfly wings and a butterfly that hung from the ceiling. The sculptor titled it "Megamorphosis." In his artist statement he said the book represented 200 million years of ginkgo knowing how to adapt and survive; the butterfly represented freedom through transformation.

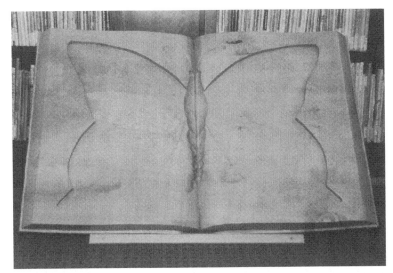

Ginkgo book

Ginkgo butterfly

I wanted to know what that meant—"freedom through transformation" —so I contacted the sculptor to meet. We sat outside a coffee shop and he rolled a cigarette. His skin was tanned and his eyes revealed depth, like he had looked inside himself for a long time.

The butterfly had many meanings, he said. "One is the transformation of the old library into the larger new one. Cutting down this tree that has 200 million years of adaptation—that represents the book itself, but we can't get access because the pages are sealed. It has more information than we do. We're cutting it down for a library, and this wood has more information, but we can't access it."

Like me, he had been following the controversy about the library renovation in the newspaper. He said, "The only way we're going to change whether we cut down a tree is by changing ourselves. It's consciousness."

෯

Chapter Eleven
THE SINGING FOREST
West Kootenays, British Columbia

For nearly a decade I had kept a yellowing magazine article about a woman who had heard a forest sing. She called it the "Singing Forest." How did it sing, I wondered. How could she hear it? Could I hear it too? Finally, I connected with Glada McIntyre by phone in April 2006.

When Glada answered the phone, she spoke in a gentle, clear voice. She described the unusual experience in June 1990, during her 18th field season of treeplanting. As she dug holes in a clearcut and filled them with seedlings, she recited the mantra—"Self emptied God filled, self emptied God filled."

She straightened herself for a moment, having been bent over the seedlings, and looked up toward the southeast. Down below, Howser Creek was collecting the melt from snow and glaciers from the North Purcell Range. The Virgin Mountain dominated the northeast vista of the valley like a pyramid. Its peak caught Glada's attention. Shafts of sunlight seemed to emanate from behind it, illuminating the slope on the other side of Howser Creek. She stood up to look closer. The trees seemed to be growing taller in the shafts of light. As she looked at the trees, she felt like she was being stretched.

"I suddenly felt about 12 feet (3.65 m) tall, and then I got this impact of sound in my solar plexus," she said. "And it grew to an upwelling, crescendo-ing hymn of praise to the Creator and joy in creation. It was absolutely unmistakable. It had nothing to do with wind in the trees. The whole slope across from me was engaged in this upwelling, crescendo-ing hymn of praise. I was quite sure that everyone else on the crew must be experiencing the same thing, that God was being revealed to us. So I called to my husband Vince, who was working beside me up the slope a ways, and said, 'Do you hear it?' He didn't hear it and wondered if I had sunstroke or something. I called to my neighbour on the other side of me, asking if he could hear it, but he didn't hear it either. I was astounded. It was so overwhelming to all the senses.

"As I was standing there feeling 12 feet tall, my whole being was being reorganized to comprehend that the planet is engaged in worship. I felt that my whole life had led up to that moment, having lived and worked in the forest and studied forest ecology at school. My whole preference for living in the woods away from civilization as much as possible seemed to suddenly make sense to me, to have led up to this moment of experiencing the entire planet as sentient and engaged in adoration. It was just a meltdown. I was just standing there with tears pouring out of me.

"And then it was as if whatever was at worship across the valley tuned in to the fact that I had tuned in to it. I got this message that seemed to be beamed directly at me. The song of joy and praise suddenly changed to a litany of sorrow. As close as my cognitive mind could translate, it said, 'Oh noble and worthy exploiters and conquerors. Have mercy. Do not end our singing, which allows your own life here.'

"Then I received what I could only describe as a molecular vision of how the forests of the planet have created and now maintain the planetary atmosphere. I was shown what must be the carbon cycle. I was aware of this incredible intelligence attempting to download information into my embryonic consciousness. I knew I could comprehend only a small part of what I was being shown. I saw how, in the forest ecosystem, there's a life force that broadcasts from some inner dimension of the mountains near the headwaters of the ecosystem. This life-force energy goes into the living water, into the air and the earth, and is received by the oldest beings in the ecosystem; here, those beings were nodes of ancient forest, which transform and then rebroadcast the energy back into the ecosystem. I saw how, when the ancient forest is removed, it plunges the ecosystem into chaos, within which ecological succession becomes unpredictable.

"I was told that mankind has removed so much of the ancient forest that it's having an incredibly difficult time maintaining the conditions necessary for life as we know it. And that we were standing at a catastrophic edge where the forest could no longer maintain the life-support systems. And that there could be an absolutely catastrophic upheaval.

"I was amazed that the forest was so polite: 'Oh noble and worthy exploiters and conquerors. Have mercy. Do not end our singing, which allows your own life here.' I wondered—Mercy? How can we have mercy? I thought mercy was God's domain to dispense. Why me? Why am I hearing this? What can I possibly do about this?

"I was told that the forest across the valley is sacred to the Holy Mother, to the Divine Spirit of Grace and Mercy. And that because it was a Japanese logging company that was cutting down the trees over there, I had to communicate with them to let them know that the forest is sacred in a way they would understand. The forest is sacred to the Goddess of Compassion, manifest as Mother Mary to Western culture, Quan Yin in the Orient, or as the Japanese know her, Kannonsama.

"As we drove out of the valley that day, I understood that I had witnessed the Song of the Planetary Forest change from a great hymn of adoration to a plea for mercy. I expected that people all over the planet must be having similar experiences."

As Glada ended her story, she sang the litany of sorrow that she had heard the forest sing: "Have mercy, have mercy, have mercy on our children." She said it haunted her for years. And then she cried because she felt she had been given a big responsibility and failed.

As she cried, my hand was gripping the phone. How could she alone have failed, I wondered, when forests were commonly viewed as board feet.

A few years later, in 1993, the company licensed to cut trees in the Howser Creek drainage advertised their plans to log the forested mountain slope that had communicated to Glada. Meadow Creek Cedar's five-year licence required it to cut 96,000 cubic metres (3.4 million cu ft) a year, and they wanted old growth. As required, the company invited public comment. Glada went to visit the Singing Forest for the first time.

The drive to the Singing Forest was a slow ascent on a logging road from the east side of Duncan Lake into the Purcell Mountains. As the road descended into the valley bottom, it followed Howser Creek heading northeast. Arriving at the foot of the mountain slope bordered by Tenise Creek, Glada hiked into the Singing Forest. She found a grove of the biggest cedar trees she had ever seen. Lichen coloured the cedars, spruce and hemlock with gold and silver. The pure mossy streams running through the forest had been undisturbed for a very long time. She took photos and left.

Back at home, Glada happened upon a column in the *Anglican Journal* written by Reverend Peter Hamel, a parish priest in Masset on Haida Gwaii. His article quoted passages from Isaiah, in which Glada recognized a description of the sentience of earth's forests that she had experienced:

You will go out in joy, and be led forth in peace; the mountains and hills will burst into song before you. . . . (Isaiah 55:12); Sing for joy, O heavens, for the Lord has done this; shout aloud, O earth beneath. Burst into song, you mountains, you forests and all your trees. . . . (Isaiah 44:23).

Rev. Hamel wrote about environmental issues for the journal. He believed that Christ died for all of creation and that Nature has rights too. So Glada called him. She asked if he knew that the passages from Isaiah that he had quoted are a contemporary phenomenon and not an historical allegory. The Reverend knew of others who had had experiences similar to Glada's, and believed they had a unique sensitivity to Nature. He flew out to meet Glada in the West Kootenays. Together they appealed the logging plans and asked that the Singing Forest be protected because of its ancient old-growth and because it had developed what they believed to be the sentient capacity to beg for mercy. They founded an ecumenical Friends of Creation Council to represent spiritual values in the land-use planning process.

Glada also organized the Applied Ecological Stewardship Coalition to represent silviculture workers, organic farmers, horse loggers, homesteaders, and sustainable foresters at the Commission on Resources and Environment (CORE). CORE aimed to resolve conflicts over land use in four major forestry regions of the province. About two-thirds of BC is forested, and the province is larger than the combined states of California, Oregon and Washington. Much of the province's economic development in the 19th and 20th centuries depended on extracting natural resources. In many rural regions, logging had been the most important employer.

By this time, Glada and her husband ended their treeplanting careers. They decided not to work in the forest industry and be in collusion with the logging of ancient forests. Living off the grid north of Argenta, in a home built from locally gathered materials, they expanded their organic farming to become a full-time livelihood.

How had people responded to Glada's claim for forest protection based on spiritual values? Protection of a forest for its biological values proved challenging enough in the history of forest conservation. A January 1995 W-FIVE, CTV Television news show answered my question.

The host of the show introduced Glada (whose name at the time was Gladys) to Canadians across the country as a "true ecozealot" who was "staking out new ground." As reporter Susan Ormiston flew with Glada to the Singing Forest, Susan noted that that it took a chopper to get there, "and after that, an open mind." Standing in the snow before a big cedar and television camera, Glada recited what the forest had said to her.

Susan commented: "But one woman's epiphany is another man's dread. The Singing Forest was supposed to be logged come spring. Gladys helped stall that." In the next scene, Susan stood with mill manager Aaron Jones who asked: "Does that mean that every forest that somebody says they had a spiritual experience in that we now can't log?"

Susan continued: Residents of the West Kootenays are used to feuding about the forests. Before the camera in Nelson, she said "one in every eight jobs are in forestry but the demographics are changing. Hippies settled here in the 1970s, stayed through the 80s, and in the 90s young urban professionals flocked here, fleeing Vancouver or Calgary. On any given day it's not hard to draw 200 people to a march for the environment. Holistic forestry has a following." Susan asked a woman at the march: "Do you think trees sing? [Woman:] "Yes they do absolutely, I've heard them myself. I sing back to them." [Man:] "Everything sings. If we didn't sing our atoms would fall apart." In the next scene, local workers in the timber industry held a rally. Their signs said: "Listen to the People."

Returning to the Singing Forest, Susan asked Glada what she thought the trees were trying to say. Glada said "There's a superphysical life force that regulates physical ecosystem processes. And that life force emanates from somewhere in the headwaters and that it's broadcast and received by the biggest oldest living beings in the drainage." Susan: "So these trees could be giant transmitters of some superphysical force?" Glada: "That's my impression. I may have simply stumbled on a place that great devas were at worship, king tree devas, mountain devas, superphysical beings of the angelic hierarchy."

"Tree devas?" remarked Susan while a logger felled a tree. "Tell that to this guy. To him a 50-foot (15.2 m) spruce means a paycheck." At the mill, Susan noted that "You won't find the usual 2 x 4s. The entire mill is calibrated to Japanese specs. Every boardfoot is exported to build homes in Japan. It meant this mill could stay open, even expand. Taiki Industry Co. of Osaka bought it five years ago and hired on 90 people. The payroll runs over $3 million."

Susan continued to comment: "Gladys' claims may have gone nowhere if it weren't for a government initiative, the Commission on Resources and Environment. Set up by the BC government, CORE, as it's known, was supposed to end the war in the woods. So here in the West Kootenays environmentalists sat down with loggers, back-to-the-landers with business people. The whole process took 18 months and cost half a million dollars. And by the time this report was written, Gladys' band of environmentalists had pushed spirituality onto the land-use agenda. Slipped it in at the round table. Most of the tough talk was on watersheds and wildlife, tourism and logging under local land-use guidelines. 'Spiritual/aesthetic' made the list."

Susan interviewed businessman Al Beix, who said he didn't expect such matters to get listed. "In the Caribou," he said, "which is another area in BC where the CORE commission had a table, they had the 'All beings' sector. When I first heard about that I thought, 'What on earth is that?' It turned out that it represents the mushrooms and the microbes. These are people speaking for the blueberries in the woods. If that's not concerning to people, I really think it should be."

The reporter interviewed the Minister of Environment. Moe Sihota said he never heard trees sing. "It may be that there's a paragraph or a line in a report that says this area should be protected because of spirituality and we'll look at it. But I will not listen for very long if someone comes in my office and says, 'Don't cut that tree Moe, because it sings.' I don't have time for that. No one should. It's flaky."

To conclude, Susan interviewed Patrick Moore, "a tree hugger who helped found Greenpeace. But when Patrick Moore left that for a consulting job with the forest industry, his former friends called him an ecojudas." Patrick summed up his view of the Singing Forest conflict for the television audience: "The biggest debate within the environmental movement is whether or not to go with this neotribal approach or to stay with a rational science based approach. That's where the division is right now. It's amazing how strong the sort of neotribal, religious kind of fervour, the cult approach, which I believe leads to a kind of ecofascism, a kind of inquisition against people who aren't ecologically correct, that sort of thing. I think it's very dangerous."

As I watched the news show, what bothered me was the ridicule. A plea for conservation of an ancient forest expressed by a metaphysical experience was portrayed as childish fantasy or worse compared to investments and paychecks.

In his CORE/West Kootenay report, Commissioner Stephen Owen said significant reductions in the annual allowable cut were actually needed to ensure a future for the industry. He recognized that thousands of jobs had been lost by more efficient harvesting and milling systems. He saw the key to prosperity to be a diversified economy, including a diversified wood products industry and retraining forest workers. The report noted that several groups at the roundtable lobbied for environmental protection. Local government asked for balance in land use, including "land-based opportunities for a broad range of spiritual, cultural, heritage, recreation, aesthetic and therapeutic pursuits." Among the concerns of the Applied Ecological Stewardship Council were small land tenures, ecosystem integrity, and protection of special significant sites. In the end, the latter got relegated to local and operational planning. The Singing Forest did not get protection.

In the meantime, Glada appealed for the forest's protection as a park, which sent scientists to survey the area's biological values. Lichenologist Trevor Goward surveyed the Tenise Creek drainage and reported on his findings to the BC government. He looked for similar stands elsewhere in the district, but couldn't find any. What he found at Tenise Creek was evidence of an "antique forest." Antique forests, he defined, occur in the toe positions of slopes where they are better protected from fire than forests on the upper slopes. Antique forests are multigenerational; whatever the age of the oldest trees, the rest of the forest predates them, perhaps by three times or more. Antique forests absorb nutrients flowing to the valley bottom, where its moist, rich soils allow for high lichen diversity. Trevor found 27 species of lichen in the Singing Forest that depend for their existence on old-growth. He considered the forest a biological archive, especially since the toe-slope positions where such forests occur are becoming rare, being productive sites for growing trees and accessible to logging: "Other places doubtless once existed in this part of the province, but I'd say they're long gone now, and not likely to return. Although one can sustainably log a mature forest, and perhaps even an old-growth forest, all you can ever do with an antique forest, besides leave it alone, is to mine it. Once it's gone, it's gone for good."

The Ministry of Forests did not view protected area status for the Singing Forest as workable in the long-term. The Ministry preferred landscape level planning for "optimizing conditions for as many species as possible (including humans)." And ecosystem management was complex and often unpredictable, and their level of knowledge was limited.

A simple solution to the controversy might have been the purchase of a section of the Singing Forest from Meadow Creek Cedar. Film star Matt Frewer, best known for his role in the TV series *Max Headroom*, offered to buy it. (Matt had purchased old maples in Ontario threatened by development and paid to have them relocated.) But the local forest district manager would not allow the company to sell its harvesting rights because the province owned the land.

Some Nelson residents who appreciated the Singing Forest's biological wealth and spiritual value took action to protect it. Matt Lowe spent many days camping out in the forest and bringing people to see it by caravan. Tamasine Drisdale collected donations for a pilgrimage to Victoria. She envisioned a thousand people walking across the province, sharing their experience of the Singing Forest and talking about old-growth forests in general, and the importance of preserving them.

"It certainly didn't live up to that," she told me, sharing her story:

"We started with 12 people walking out of the forest including a senior and a couple of children. People were always joining or dropping off. In Vancouver a man in a wheelchair joined us, and he wheeled for the last week all across Vancouver Island. It took a whole month to do it and we were pressed for time to get to Victoria before papers were signed to allow the clearcutting. We hoped to get an audience with the ministers."

They met with deputy ministers instead. Then the Ministry of Forest approved the cutting permit.

Those who had been working on the campaign decided to do spiritual witnessing on the first day of logging. "About 30 people went up there that night and talked around the campfire about what that was," Tamasine recalled. "It was nonintervention. You are not to obstruct what's going on. You're there to observe with an open heart and be honest about your feelings. And then the next morning another carload of people came up, and with them was this one guy who really did not understand what spiritual witnessing was. While all the people were gathering around at the bottom where we were asked to stand to be out of the way of logging, singing, praying, holding space, just preparing ourselves for being there, just watching what was going to go on, this guy argued with the loggers, and pressed the point that he's not leaving until they get a legal injunction prohibiting him from being there."

At that point Tamasine withdrew from what became a blockade because that wasn't in line with her spiritual beliefs. From Glada's experience of the Singing Forest, she understood the forest to be the embodiment of Kuan Yin, the goddess of compassion. "For me it awakened my compassion for all beings, including the loggers, including those who were trying to care for their families, and that what was going on there in the forest wasn't just a plea to save the trees. It was a plea for compassion, and that would only come about when people experience it in their real lives. For me the starting place for that is between ourselves. If you can't recognize my humanity and show compassion for me on that level, how are you going to recognize it in a tree or a shrub or in a rock or in a river?"

As I listened to Tamasine's story, I thought it odd to have compassion for a rock, even if it might be possible to have compassion for a tree or a forest. But then, I am a member of a Western industrial society, whose science and major religions have separated humans from the rest of Nature, as though we are not a part of it.

An injunction was enforced that prohibited people from being present when the Singing Forest was logged. Tamasine contacted Meadow Creek Cedar to ask if she could visit the forest before it was logged. "I did not want to violate any injunction. The mill manager told me that I could be there during nonlogging hours, which were 6 o' clock in the evening to 6 o'clock in the morning. So I arranged to go up with the man in the wheelchair and a few others to do a night vigil there, and basically to pray for compassion, that that be the result of things that had gone on up there.

"We lit our fire on the roadside, and the man in the wheelchair stayed down at a camp where the people had been blockading. In the morning, just as we were putting our fire out and cleaning up the area to be ready to leave by 6 o'clock, at about a quarter to, a bunch of trucks came barreling up the hill."

Tamasine and companions were arrested. They got out of jail by the afternoon. The officers found the man in the wheelchair and gave him a lift to town. After the forest was logged, Tamasine went to see it.

She felt a tremendous loss for the forest and for the people who tried to do something different there. "It was a real leap of faith in humility," she said "for people to try to defend this forest on the grounds of spiritual values, being white people who don't have a history on this land that goes back any more than a few hundred years. It was a very profound statement. We really went out on a limb to uphold our right to be taken seriously as people who used the land for our spiritual practice."

In 1995, Meadow Creek Cedar felled sections of old-growth on the mountain slope where the Singing Forest once sang. In 2004 the company received approval to log more of it. In 2005, the Japanese sold the company. By 2007, a third permit would approve more logging, resulting in a total logged area of about 200 hectares (494 acres). A narrow strip of land beside Tenise Creek, and another small patch southwest—all 162 hectares (400 acres) of it—were conserved for the time being. The forest district called it an OGMA, an old-growth management area, mostly because the soils were wet and the land unstable. OGMAs were not permanent and did not confer protection. The guidelines encouraged OGMAs in as much of the "inoperable" forest as possible, that is, inaccessible areas not profitable to log. The Kootenay Lake Forest District could not justify conserving most of the old-growth in the Singing Forest when there were better or equivalent stands throughout the district.

In the summer of 2006 I went to see the Singing Forest for myself—what was left of it. On the way, I attended a meeting of the Inland Temperate Rainforest (ITR) coalition, to which Glada had invited me.

Among some conservationists and scientists, the ITR was becoming recognized as a globally unique ecosystem—unique because it's an inland temperate rainforest, not a coastal one. Its antique forests, growing in place for more than 1000 years, have produced several old cedars over 2000 years old. The ITR included high-elevation areas as well as valleys

Clearcut
of the
Singing
Forest

with a rich variety of tree-dwelling lichen feeding mountain caribou, also unique to this region. ITR proponents claimed the region stretched as far north as Prince George, BC and south into Idaho, Montana and Washington, for a total of 14 million hectares (34.6 million acres). The BC government referred to its part of the ITR as the interior wetbelt or interior cedar-hemlock forest—a region that produces a lot of commercial timber because it's wet like the coast.

Enroute to the ITR meeting in Silverton, I followed the Silvery Slocan Circle Tour, locally promoted for visitors to the West Kootenays. I passed postcard-pretty valleys defined by vertical rock mountainsides and littered with crumbling mines, tailing heaps and abandoned railways. Arriving at the meeting place, the Silverton Gallery, I parked in a lot beside a neatly tended green lawn where machines from the mining era proudly stood. I thought it an odd display for a meeting about conservation, but true to context for a region that paralleled the 19th century rush for resources throughout the Pacific Northwest.

Inside the meeting hall, people were milling about or sitting at tables set in a semi-circle. Someone told me that Glada had not yet arrived, so I sat down at a table beside the representative for the World Temperate Rainforest Network. She too had heard a tree speak, which sent her on a mission of forest conservation. Marilyn James sat nearby. She represented the Sinixt, an officially extinct tribe in Canada. Lance Craighead sat at the table's end; he came from a distinguished family of wildlife biologists known for their grizzly bear research. A member of Valhalla Wilderness Society stood up and introduced Lance, who would speak about the conservation design for the ITR.

Affable, articulate and thorough, Lance described in detail the state of wildlife habitat in the ITR for grizzlies, wolverines, lynx, cougars, wolves, and mountain caribou. He said it was fragmented. Wildlife needed over half of the ITR protected from development. They needed corridors to roam because populations that are not isolated have a greater chance of survival. The mountain caribou needed large areas of old forest to survive; they roam through the high, mid and low elevations of the region throughout the seasons. During the winter they eat tree lichens, which grow in sufficient quantity on trees at least 100 years old.

At some point during Lance's presentation, Glada had arrived. I noticed her sitting at a table without pen, pencil, map, or paper. When she got up to walk by a window, I watched how the sunlight lit up her white-blonde hair. Her summer dress accented her petite frame. She was short. From time to time she left and returned to the room. I imagined her to go outside to sit under an old tree, which is what I wanted to do.

A representative of the Species at Risk Coordination Office (SARCO) spoke. He admitted that the caribou had fallen through the cracks of the 2003 Species at Risk Act. Even though the scientists were unanimous, he said, that continuing with existing land use plans would threaten the species' survival, current land use plans would all be honoured.

Glada retorted: "Our work here represents to the world the value of maintaining this globally unique inland temperate rainforest, not a single species within it, but a full complement that adds up to biological integrity of the functioning ecosystem of the inland rainforest. It doesn't seem that the focus the government has on caribou is reflective of or respectful of the unique value of the inland rainforest. Or the global significance of the immediate risk of the entire region to the planet."

The SARCO rep didn't know if the region had global significance. Mounting agitation produced a flutter of raised hands. Marilyn suggested they file an international joint commission for the protection and management of the caribou. "That's the only way we're going to impact anything," she said. "We've been talking for years. Nobody's getting anywhere."

Another voice shot out: "While we talk, the forest falls. We talk and the forest falls. I'll drive away from this meeting and I'll see two or three logging trucks, and they're going all the time."

The SARCO rep put his finger on a crack in the bursting dam: "You know amongst your own groups how difficult it is to come upon some kind of unity of purpose. It's taken you a long time to get to the point where you're all collaborating." The room became silent, but not for long.

Despite a general climate of intemperate remarks, I returned to the meeting the next day. Disagreement ensued over the definition of old growth trees. Valhalla Wilderness Society promoted a declaration calling for a ban on old growth logging. Biologists disliked the proposed 140-year age limit for old growth; it's the diversity of old-growth structure that matters, not age, they argued. Glada remarked that cottonwoods get old at 60 to 80 years, and that a thermal regulatory definition of big trees might be more effective. She mentioned something about higher planetary vibrations as well that I didn't understand.

When we broke for lunch I sat with Marilyn outside. She saw Glada's role as a really difficult one "because of the playground she plays in." On the one hand, there's Glada's science knowledge, she said. "People can acknowledge that she knows what she's talking about because she studied the documents, she understands what they're saying. But in terms of the environmental movement, when you're talking science at a table, she has these other experiences that she tries to infuse into the conversation. There's not many scientists who have those kind of experiences to relate to it, so then it just becomes eye-ball rolling and very dismissive of what this landscape has to offer us."

Marilyn was the official spokesperson for the Sinixt, who numbered 6800 on both sides of the border, she said. "We truly believe we're all spiritual beings. And when we can relate to this landscape in a much more evolved way, respectful, in that we have reverence for rocks, reverence for trees, reverence for water, these things can teach us, you know. And we're open to those teachings. And those teachings are every bit as viable and sometimes way more viable than what science can ever offer in terms of landscape explanation, landscape experience, landscape value."

"So you're saying that when she talks about her spiritual experience, it's counterproductive?" I asked.

"Right. Not to me because I understand it. I think they don't understand it. It might not even be an eye-ball rolling thing. It's off the charts. Glada's experiences don't even blip on most of these guys' radar. And I'm not saying they all disregard it. On some level they have those experiences, but right away it gets put into how they can rationalize, how to create logic around it, how to create an explanation—'Well you know with old growth, when the trees split open and there's a split in the shaft of the wood and a little of this decomposing centre of the tree and the wind hits it just right, that's what makes the noise. It's not a Singing Forest.'"

I had noticed that people who rolled their eyes about the Singing Forest assumed trees needed vocal cords to sing.

The ITR meeting was over and Glada was leading me to the Singing Forest. The sky was blue and a dump of rain settled the dust on logging roads. The vistas of snow-capped forested mountains refreshed me as we drove. Entering the clearcuts, the temperature began to rise.

Glada
McIntyre

Heading down into the valley bottom, I could see The Virgin Mountain dominate the northeast vista. The Singing Forest mountain slope appeared in the southeast. The logging road continued to descend as it followed Howser Creek. We parked on the road beside a toe slope of the Singing Forest mountain that had not been logged. Glada darted into the forest. I followed her into a grove of old cedars

Gaps of sunlight, filtered by fans of cedar needles, lit my steps among the big, medium and small trees. Needles caught by spider webs whirled between trees. Devil's club arched over ferns and berry bushes. Each step I took slightly bounced on the floor of moss. Lime-green lichen coloured the bark of big cedars. I saw Glada through the trees leaning against a big old cedar. She seemed to be listening. I listened too but heard only branches crack beneath my feet. I found an old cedar to lean against. The whole grove was silent. I found myself listening to the stillness itself, sensing a life-force.

We lingered for a while and then left. We drove to the mountain's southwesterly aspect, where a long swathe of forest had been clearcut. We parked and Glada bounded across the clearcut like the agile treeplanter she once was. Fortunately she wore a red rain jacket so that I could follow her in the bush that was three to four feet (.9 to 1.2 m) deep and full of berries. I could not see where to put my feet, but could feel the stumps and debris that turned this place into a wooden mine field, especially on sloping ground. Below the brush were branches that had once burned sharp in heaps of smoking slash among thighs of ripped wooden fibre. I looked up to find Glada. She was looking down into the debris, moving here and there, as though she was looking for something she had lost. She appeared very sad, as though grieving the loss of relations who were slain.

ɞ♥

Chapter Twelve
DIALOGUE GROVES
Upper Mattole River Watershed, California

S ome say the Mattole means clear water. Others say it means crystal in the language of the Mattole people who once lived and fished in the Mattole River watershed. Oldtimers recall that the river carried salmon so thick you could step on their backs to cross it. Before logging, these parts of California's north coast were continuously cloaked by canopy, which kept the river cool for salmon to spawn. Today less than eight percent remains of virgin old-growth forest in a watershed of 304 square miles (787.3 sq km) within the Northern Coast Ranges bordered by the Pacific Coast. Were it not for two generations of back-to-the-landers and Cistercian nuns with a land ethic, more temperate rainforest and giant redwoods would be lost.

It was June 2002 when I entered a forest of this watershed that had inspired its conservation. From Highway 101 to Redway, I followed the circuitous Briceland-Thorn Road into the ridges and valleys of the Coast Ranges toward the Lost Coast. Thickets of Douglas-firs and tan oaks lined the road, decorated here and there with tattooed hippie vans. The occasional school bus with a smoke stack sat in the woods between homesteads. After Thorn Junction, the road paralleled the Mattole River and led me through the town of Whitethorn to Ancestor Grove where I parked in a grass meadow. People arrived, parked and waited. When Rondal Snodgrass arrived, he hugged everyone. He was tall, thin and likeable. He had retired from being executive director of the local land trust organization Sanctuary Forest. Today he would lead us on a history hike into the headwaters of the Matttole River—*the* Sanctuary Forest.

As we walked from Ancestor Grove into the woods, Rondal stopped

139

beside a gently flowing creek. "McNasty Creek was named after a landowner who lived here," he said. Rondal explained that neighbours called him McNasty because he blocked the shortcut trail into town that traversed his property. I looked behind a thicket of shrubs and trees where an old wooden homestead continued to crumble; nearby, a cement fire pit would outlast it. Decorating the firepit were large abalone shells as rare as old growth.

"I'm not sure every detail is true," said Rondal, his gray-blue eyes twinkling beneath a shock of white hair. "There were a lot of false claims on the land where we stand. Trucks and equipment would arrive and trees would disappear. Chuck Hall is most notorious. He logged a lot of Whale Gulch in the back trail without ownership. When he was discovered as a criminal, he fled to Canada and they caught him at the border. The back trail from Whitethorn to Whale Gulch was called Hall Road. For a long time I thought it stood for h-a-u-l!"

Someone asked Rondal about the ribbons tied to some of the branches that brushed us as we pressed into the thickness of forest. Rondal said they meant that someone had been in the forest. Ribbon colours meant certain things in logging operations, like blue for roads or skid trails. In Sanctuary Forest, the white ribbons helped to reflect flashlights for moon-lit hikes, he said.

Rondal took to the upward winding trail like a fish in water or like an Indian elder, barefoot in boots. I spied wild ginger, rhododendrons, a Calypso orchid, and lavender. A spring gurgled along the trail and a creek ran so clear I could see the small fry of steelhead or coho. Rondal stopped. He said the creek had once been filled with silt, rocks and broken branches—the usual debris from clearcutting that prevented salmon from reproducing. He said the spring was sacred and invited us to talk to it. He asked someone to be the spring and someone to speak to the spring.

Someone ventured: "Where are you coming from, Spring? Where are you going?"

We waited for an answer. I heard only the sound of water trickling over rocks. Then we chuckled like the trickling spring.

"First dialogue!" laughed Rondal. "Thank you spring, thank you humans!"

As we trekked uphill, some identified the trees we passed: madrone (arbutus), chinquapin, Douglas-fir, and yews. When we passed by a tall tan oak Rondal paused and said, "I saw lightning strike that tree. It spiralled round the trunk, right down into the ground, then the crown just lit up like a ball of fire." We examined the tree. It looked to be alive.

We followed several switch-back trails to hike up the mountainside. A giant redwood named Big Red loomed above us. Big Red had been saved from logging by the conservation of this forest. Rondal explained that before World War II, this watershed had been mostly intact, with virgin Douglas-fir and redwoods populating the headwaters. After the war it was stripped, leaving uncut patches here and there. I began to realize how this history hike was helping put the forest back together—through the minds and hearts of the people. Describing the forest as a place of stories was giving it history that protected its heritage, and gave it a future.

In a clearing we stopped to rest, although Rondal did not seem tired. "Welcome to Dialogue Grove," he said. "Go and hug a tree." Our puzzled faces half-smiled. Had Rondal not been so child-like (or a "spontaneous being," as somebody whispered), I would have ignored him. But I gave in to the fun of it and found a tree to sit beside. Rondal coaxed us: "Let it embrace you." I participated in the exercise self-consciously. I smiled at the name of a place I thought was spelled Dial-a-log Grove.

Rondal Snodgrass
leaning on Big Red

Rondal knew what it was like to be embraced by a tree. He had been living in the Mattole for some time when rumours about the existence of a big redwood were circulating. Others had seen the tree somewhere, sort of nearby, on a ridge. The mystery of this tree lingered on, teasing the imagination to contemplate a survivor of the Logging Age until Rondal could bear it no more. He determined to find the tree. On a second attempt in the summer of 1986, he found Big Red marked with a red ribbon.

At the time of finding the tree, Rondal was struck by a tremendous sadness that he felt: "I had some tears that were unexpected, and tears were not easy for me to experience. I felt a kind of energy and left with a desperate, forlorn feeling that how tragic this would be for the tree to be cut. It had been marked at that point with a red ribbon, which every tree in the forest had—it was a 100 percent cruise of the area. On going home, in the next few weeks, frequently near dawn I had a sensation of contact with the tree calling for help."

In the summer of 1986 another local went hiking in the woods. He too found a red ribbon on Big Red and other trees and plucked them off, filling up a shopping bag full.

"What do I do with these?" he asked a nun at the door of Redwoods Monastery, a place where people brought their souls for healing and their questions too. Its 300-plus acres (121.4 ha) of meadows and old-growth sat below Big Red, who presided on a mountain ridge overlooking the monastery. These Cistercians were nuns and stewards of their land. They valued the solitude and beauty of the forest. Outside their chapel's ceiling-to-floor picture window stood four big redwoods that were growing together.

The nuns offered a place for locals to meet about the red ribbons. They thought the Collins Pine Company land would always be safe from logging; but now, six old-growth parcels totalling 1200 acres (485.6 ha) were up for sale. At the meeting they talked about ways to save the forests. Myriam Dardenne, founder and abbess of the monastery, valued the redwoods as cathedrals in their own right. Being from Belgium, she came to understand that America valued the primacy of private property. She said the only way to save the forest was to buy it.

Rondal gasped: "I thought we would try to influence the owners to manage it differently or stop them from what I thought was destructive logging practices through direct action. I was a product of the Civil Rights movement and spent a number of years working for the Student Nonviolent Coordinating Committee. We weren't going to buy Mississippi to make sure blacks could vote."

The prospect of land purchase was daunting. For two parcels for sale (280 acres [113.3 ha] where Big Red stood and an 80-acre (32.3-ha) parcel they called Dreamstream), the ad hoc group would have to raise a three-percent security deposit to make a bid of $1.5 million. They all wondered where the money would come from. They decided to trust.

In 1987 the group founded a non-profit organization called Sanctuary Forest, Inc. after the forest and tree that inspired them. To raise money to buy the land, volunteers produced a brochure. Mailing lists were donated and the three-percent security deposit arrived. But Eel River Sawmills in partnership with Barnum Timber won the bid for all 1200 acres (485.6 ha).

Sanctuary Forest persisted. A delegation went to visit the president of Eel River Sawmills. Would he agree, they asked, to sell the two parcels if an upcoming state proposition passed? In June 1988, Californians voted to conserve coastal land by a state bond, with $4 million going to the Mattole. But Eel River Sawmills held on to the land. By the fall, loggers arrived to fell trees at Vista Ridge across the road from the monastery.

As a matter of policy, Sanctuary Forest had decided not to litigate or engage in direct action, but to negotiate instead to develop friendly relations with the neighbours. Others outside the organization decided to pursue a confrontational route. When loggers entered the town of Whitethorn, they drove beneath a banner that stretched across main street. It read: "Free the Mattole. Stop the clearcutting."

Rondal looked down the road and saw a group of ragtag soldiers: "It looked like this painting of the Revolutionary War where someone is playing the flute and someone's carrying the flag." Earth First! had come to town.

Four miles away, about 50 local people stood between the loggers and the trees, blocking a newly cut road. "I didn't expect as many people," said a logger who waited patiently while munching an apple. "The lungs of our planet are being clearcut," shouted a young girl. Debate ensued between the factions. A teacher from Whale Gulch School introduced the children to a logger, who explained that he cut down trees for a living, five days a week. The children asked about the animals, about the fish. The loggers grouped to strategize and the locals linked hands to sing "We shall not be moved." Some slept in the forest that night.

On day two of the protest, four women, three men and two girls were arrested. Security officers handcuffed women clinging to a tree and pulled men from a bulldozer. People scattered and some climbed into the canopy to watch the loggers fell between 20 to 50 trees—a count that depended on which side you were on. Just in time the tension broke when news of a court order arrived to halt the logging—for awhile. During this time, Sanctuary Forest tried to keep the peace by holding vigils. When the loggers showed up at dawn, they found people standing around a fire in prayer.

By 1990, 80 acres (32.4 ha) on Vista Ridge were clearcut and a logging road planned to Big Red. In the meantime, a local teacher took a class to visit the tree. When the class returned to school, students wrote about their experiences. One student said she couldn't understand why so much care and money was given to saving dinosaur bones, things that were dead, when a tree in their forest was living over 2000 years.

As Sanctuary Forest continued to negotiate for land, Rondal began to see the representatives of public agencies as people but resented their agencies. In time, he came to see that most agencies and corporations were just groups of people. Rondal became Sanctuary Forest's first executive director. The monastery taught him not to burn bridges: "You're just going to get isolated if you burn a bridge. You burn a bridge if you condemn a person as guilty. You're not going to do business with them and they're not going to do business with you."

It took some time to build bridges however. Some families in Whitethorn Valley like the Barnums made their living by logging. In the beginning they didn't want to talk with Sanctuary Forest about protecting the land, and Barnum Timber and Eel River Sawmills never did sell Big Red and Dreamstream to Sanctuary Forest. In 1989, the Wildlife Conservation Board (WCB) bought Big Red's parcel, and then Save-the-Redwoods League bought Dreamstream and sold it to WCB. By the end of 1990, Sanctuary Forest had conserved 700 acres (283.3 ha) by conservation easements and agreements with private and public landowners. Nine years later, 3500 acres (1416.4 ha) of old growth were protected by acquisition; 6000 more acres (2428 ha) were protected by conservation easements; and the national nonprofit Trust for Public Land awarded Sanctuary Forest its first annual Land Trust Achievement Award for innovative, consensus-building, partnership protection of the Mattole River headwaters. By 2003 and $22 million of donations later, Sanctuary Forest had preserved over 10,400 acres (4208.7 ha) of forest and open space in the Mattole watershed.

In celebration of those who have donated to the land trust, Sanctuary Forest holds a Naming Ceremony every year in the fall. I attended in September 2002 on the autumn equinox. We entered Ancestor Grove at dusk and took our seats in a circle around a fire. Someone played guitar. Someone else played the flute. We held candles. Lists of names of annual and honorary donors were passed from hand to hand, and we read all the names. Then the lists were burned in the fire. We watched the smoke and ashes of the names float upward into the trees, as though the spirits of the people blended into the life force of the forest.

Like Rondal, another local had been entranced by the legend of Big Red, and determined to find the tree:

"If the earth has a belly button, the Wall probably grows out of it," wrote Bill Jackson in the *Redwood Record*. "Before we first entered the grove where the Wall lived, me and my guide, I had been given the usual preparation. I had been told that the Wall would be different. I had been told that the Wall would be unlike any tree I had ever seen ever, etc. And, like all new Wall-viewers, I had pointed to the many giant redwood trees that dotted the trail on the way to the Wall and I had asked if they were the Wall. My guide ignored my questions. Then, when we had finally neared the actual base of the tree itself, everything had begun to change. The forest floor had become more spongy and it was littered with redwood needles that were longer, fatter, and wider than the usual redwood needles. An eerie stillness had begun to pervade the air. I can remember looking at my guide with a question on my face. My guide returned my glance with an icy look of pale humility. It was then that I knew that we were in the 'presence.' It was then that I first gazed up into the Wall. It was then that I experienced a head-rush. It was then that I fell out."

It was late August when Richard and I went to find Big Red. We picked up Jim who was on retreat at Redwoods Monastery. My husband Richard knew the monastery land, being the monastery's honorary forester, so we trusted him as our guide on a path rarely traveled, which was not a road or even a trail. He decided to take the back way into Sanctuary Forest through monastery grounds. Jim looked forward to the adventure while I wished I had a compass and topographic map.

The back way into the forest began with crawling under thorny bushes. Then rain set in. Even with raingear, we got wet from the inside out. We scouted for game trails to get out of the bush, and followed Yew Creek where yews were really plentiful. I spied white ribbons that seemed to mark the trail.

Richard looked across the creek. "There's the direct path to Big Red," he said, "but it's a hellova hike."

I looked up at the steep slope without toeholds or branches to grip. "Why don't we follow the ribbons?" I said.

Richard looked up the slope and back at me, furrowing his brow. "Alright," he said, "but I don't know where that trail leads." We followed the white ribbons until they disappeared. Then Richard crossed Yew Creek, not looking back at us, and scaled the steep slope. Jim and I had no choice but to follow.

Halfway up I dug in my heels in the scrabble. "How much further?" I asked. Richard ignored me. When we reached the top of the ridge I asked the same question.

"Just keep to the ridgetop," he said.

"What ridgetop?" Looking around in the four directions I saw only an elevated ocean of thick fog.

Richard looked cross. "You just have to trust me," he said.

"It's not that I don't trust you," I retorted. "It's that I want to know where I am. How do you know we're going in the right direction?"

"Dead reckoning," he said, the two words rippling into the space between us like rocks thrown into a lake.

Dead reckoning? I thought. Was that some kind of internal compass? Perhaps, but only a fool would follow a dedicated bushwacker. Mounting anxiety made me shiver as much as the wet clothes sticking to my body. "We're lost," I said. "Look, even the animals know better than to come here—there's no game trail!"

"Want to turn back?" Richard half-smiled and turned into the bush, demonstrating forest calisthenics—getting down on all fours, rising to straddle blowdown, and ripping sagging raingear. I cursed under my breath. Jim made no comment.

Minutes or hours passed on this course. Then Jim shouted: "We found the trail!" White ribbons reappeared as suddenly as they had disappeared. Jim led us into a thicket of tan oaks and then into a swale. Big Red shot up like the water from a whale's spout.

Looking upward into the fog, I could see no branches on her trunk. I had been told that the top of this 200-foot (60.9-m) giant had been blown off, and yet she towered above the canopy, a canopy I could not even see. Just as her swale of tan oaks had its own character—the tangle of branches on sloping ground, the thick litter of leaves and needles, the stillness of a sacred chamber—Big Red had a forceful personality. She spoke by her density and dogged resistance to fire and chainsaw. Looking downward, I followed her clubfoot grip on the earth. At the base of a small charred cave a few branches formed steps to an altar. On the altar had been set a postcard-size drawing of a hand, within which swirled forest plants and animals—the logo of Sanctuary Forest.

Big Red

In 1993, Catherine Allport had a vision: "Return the land to the land in the name of women. By doing so, the trees will give you energy for your activism, however that is manifested." Immediately after the vision, she spoke about it to others, and continued to do so to anyone who would listen, never asking anyone for money. In a matter of weeks, she had the down payment for 14 acres (5.6 ha) in the Mattole River watershed with a $180,000-price tag.

A month before her vision, Rondal had shown her and other women the 14-acre parcel. Sanctuary Forest had purchased it in 1992, the strategy being to buy land and resell it with conservation easements. This acreage was remarkable for its two old-growth redwoods standing side-by-side, in one of the few redwood groves remaining beside the Mattole River.

In 1994 the Women's Forest Sanctuary nonprofit land trust named the forest after itself. The mission was "to return the land to the land as an act of healing and reconciliation with Nature, and to create a sanctuary space where women and their allies can hear the wisdom of the ancient forest and where the sacred feminine can arise in all." By 2003, after nine years of fundraising campaigns mostly in San Francisco and Berkeley, the original mortgage was paid off, leaving friends and founders to be paid back for their loans.

In the summer of 2003, Catherine invited me to attend the third annual Women's Forest Sanctuary retreat at the Sacred Grove. She had gone every year, she told me, and the sensations of the forest stayed with her: "It's like taking a giant vitamin."

Finding the Women's Forest Sanctuary was easier than finding Big Red, although I backtracked a couple of times on Briceland-Thorn Road, looking for something of a sign. What I found was a string of cowrie shells hung from a spike on a nurse log inside a pull-out. I assumed this female symbol of goddess protection to mark the spot. I parked under the trees and wandered into a grove. Two big redwoods stopped me in my tracks. I guessed they were old, about 1000 or 2000 years old. Because redwoods rise up from their buttresses without much of a taper, they reminded me of ancient Greek columns.

I looked around. The grandmother trees had shed thick, sharp branches in a storm that now pierced the forest floor. I wandered over to a grove nearby. Another big redwood had been struck by lightning that ripped off about 60 feet (18.3 m) of its bark that laid on the ground. I poked around. The outhouse toilet was full. The roof on the only wooden structure needed repair. Slash had been piled here and there. I found the Mattole River on the edge of the groves. It ran so clear I could see small fry, and I reflected. This crystal clarity was not to be taken for granted. It resulted from the perseverance of many to conserve these forests. I sat by the river, poking my toes in the water and felt refreshed.

By the afternoon, a few cars of women arrived. I helped them haul their gear and set up camp. They had come from the Bay Area. Some were activists and some were Women's Forest Sanctuary organizers. Catherine had been a photojournalist in South Africa for nine years. Meave O'Connor was a Berkeley activist and special education teacher. Meave told me that last summer the women held a work party in the grove. They leased a chipper and cut up the windthrow, but the chipper was too loud and violent. Catherine agreed. There was no money for forest management, but there was no stress around that. A guiding principle of caretaking was: "If it wants to continue, it will continue."

In the evening we ate a fancy dinner, prepared by recipes the women talked about. As we sat around the campfire, Catherine said, "We used to do a lot more. We used to do big events in the Bay Area. But since I and others moved, that's kind of dwindled down, and now we basically hardly do anything. Every once in a while someone will come along and want to do a benefit. We had a benefit in Santa Fe. We sent out letters. Now it's gotten down to twice a year. We have to raise the money to continue to pay off the loan. It always comes. It always comes in exactly the right amount or more. I sat at a table and did a Mother's Day event in Santa Fe next to the Forest Guardians, and people came by and I gave them flyers, and someone gave us $25,000. It's like, great. That's just how it works. Nobody is attached to this. Those trees wanted us to do this. We're doing it, that's all. I am really interested in doing nothing. That's my direction. I like the fact that I am part of a little organization that does nothing."

The next day we took a hike. Along the way Meave told me how the forest nurtures her: "When I get tired, when I need inspiration, I just travel back to the grove. I go there in my consciousness. I can see and smell it. I sit under those grandmother trees and call down their strength. The trees continue to remind me of how important it is to approach activism from a place of love and with an open heart." This sentiment was a legacy of Sanctuary Forest.

In the morning of the third day, Meave asked to read to us a tree meditation that she had written. We were keen to listen and everyone found a tree to lean upon. Meave called it "Grounding and Growing the Force of Compassion":

Sit in a comfortable position, close your eyes and begin to breathe slowly and deeply, breathing the deep breath of the belly. Feel yourself beginning to relax as you breathe. Become refreshed with each breath and feel your worries floating away. Begin to feel yourself becoming stronger and more focused with each breath.

And as you breathe imagine that your spine is the trunk of a mighty redwood tree and extend your roots down into the earth. As your roots go deeper, notice how they begin to intertwine with the roots of other trees, not only with the roots around you, but also with many of the tree roots around the planet. Continue to intertwine your roots with the roots of our many kindred spirits who, like us, hope to grow a new and more loving and compassionate culture. Like the mighty redwood trees, as we embrace one another with our roots, our collective force starts to become even stronger and more open to love.

As we breathe we take up the energy and love from our collective root structure. We send this force up through our bodies to the top of our heads, where it is sent up to connect to the glow of love and protection that has always surrounded the Earth, but is becoming stronger now because we need its energy and inspiration more than ever.

As you touch in with this beautiful glow of light, take some of it down with your next exhalation, down through your body and through your root system to where you embrace the other roots. As we continue this rhythm, our collective root structure also begins to put off a glow of energy as it grows stronger, and other roots slowly begin to come down below the surface of the Earth to join us as an ever increasing presence of love and compassion.

And as we continue with each inhalation, we take up our collective intentions for the planet through our bodies and up to the ever glowing light. And with our exhalation we continue to bring some of that light down through our bodies as we connect to our ever stronger root system.

We bring up our vision with each inhale and we bring down the inspiration to fulfill that vision with our exhale. And as we continue to breathe deeply, feel how our roots and even our branches intertwine, and the power weaves through and dances among us like the wind. Feel it moving.

Relax, while breathing in the power that Mother Earth has provided for us. And when you are ready, open your eyes and be here now.

When I opened my eyes, I felt connected to the forest and strengthened by that connection.

For the remainder of the morning, we packed our gear to leave. I remembered Rondal coaxing me to hug a tree, and how self-conscious I had felt. So it surprised me that I suggested to the women that we sit around a grandmother tree before we leave. Everyone thought it was a good idea.

We sat with our spines erect, our backs pressing against the trunk that we encircled. The only sounds to be heard apart from swatting insects, scratching bites and the flitting of insect wings, were the dropping of needles from the redwoods. As I continued to press against the grandmother, I felt my heart beat harder. I breathed in more deeply until it felt as though I was breathing through a hole in my chest. I felt lighter and more peaceful. And then I realized that I had dialed a tree.

৪৯

Chapter Thirteen
OPA
Bowen Island, British Columbia

On a morning ferry crossing Howe Sound, I looked out upon the water. It was mid-February 2006 and time for a retreat.

Arriving at the ferry terminal on Bowen Island I drove onto the main street. Along the way stood restored historic buildings and tasteful mini-malls. The place looked upscale, or like "sophisticated rural living," according to a Bowen Island brochure on the ferry. People can live in the country and commute for work in Vancouver, said the brochure. The island is 20 minutes by ferry from Horseshoe Bay and 30 minutes more from downtown Vancouver, depending on the traffic. Also called the "people's playground," Bowen Island had long been popular for summer holidays. During the first half of the 1900s, the Union Steamship Company purchased a resort, built a dance pavilion, and lured Vancouverites on board to enjoy the island pleasures. Behind the tended, pleasant landscapes, loggers and farmers cleared the land.

Today the island attracted visitors to its spas, art galleries, marinas, and restaurants. Xenia Centre attracted people too, which is where I headed. A popular retreat centre for personal renewal, it was also home to a 1000-year-old Douglas-fir that survived extensive island logging. The tree was called Opa, which means grandfather in German.

From main street I drove north into Crippen Regional Park and then turned onto Smith Road—likely named after early homesteaders. At the end of the road I drove into the Centre. Passing fenced turf for horses and the beginnings of a stable, I noticed stumps among the shrubs. I parked near a footpath to the Centre lodge and followed it.

I met no one inside the lodge, so I wandered through it, admiring the restoration of an old log home. Entering the kitchen, I looked out the window at a large meadow. Lining an edge of the meadow were what appeared to be retreat accommodations—a renovated barn and chicken coup and a few yurts. A very tall spruce commanded the middle of the meadow, surrounded by more tall trees. One big hemlock piqued my curiosity. I left the lodge to inspect it. What had looked like one hemlock was six growing from one large stump.

I walked beyond a central meadow, where trees, stumps, and trees growing on stumps shrouded a trail into the woods. The trail invited me to hike all the way to Killarney Lake and back. By the time I returned to Xenia's open meadow, I had counted 55 stumps upon which trees were growing. Restoration was happening in this place. Seeing all those stumps reclaimed by Nature improved my mood and gave me hope.

I returned to pass the lodge and walked along the entrance road. A sign near a small grove of young alders said "Opa." I passed under a driftwood archway onto a raised walkway and stood there, beholding a very old and large Douglas-fir. Fire had scorched the lower trunk and left its mark. But what stood out were the cuts. On the trunk a few feet above my head were two cuts—a wedge cut (perhaps intended as a back cut) that had healed, and a foot below that, a thin slice, also healed. I stepped off the walkway and walked around the trunk to discover a longer horizontal cut. Perhaps all these cuts were made at different times. But it was clear that intent to fell the tree had been abandoned.

I returned to the walkway to notice a bench built with back support that tilted backward for support to look upward into the tree. The walkway did not encircle the tree but continued a short way beyond it. Near the walkway on the ground rested one of Opa's thick shoulder branches where it had fallen. Around the tree lay remains of other trees—more stumps and a fallen tree that been girdled with a chain that still hugged its trunk.

I sat down upon the bench and leaned back to gaze into the canopy for what seemed to be a long time.

Later that day, I met Angelyn Toth. She stood beside her horse near the larger meadow, stroking it and talking with a few people. Shorter than average height and petite, with shoulder-length, blonde hair framing her round eyes, she talked about her horse. I listened and observed. I detected a British accent. Angelyn asked the man to take the horse, and invited me inside her home, beyond the public area. Once inside, we sat in warmth and comfort, amid the artsy, rustic, wooden decor popular among island dwellers. She told me how she bought this place.

She had a vision for years of having a retreat centre, she said. She could afford to buy about two acres. When a realtor showed her this

Entrance
to Opa

former sheep farm in disrepair on Bowen Island, they discovered Opa on the property. "I felt like falling to my knees," she recalled.

"There was a time when I let it go, thinking it was a crazy idea because I couldn't find a way to do it. Then one night I had a dream. I remember getting the message that I have to buy this land because of the tree. The message was that it hasn't fulfilled its purpose yet; it's not ready to be taken down. At the time, developers were interested in subdividing the land. I felt responsible for the tree."

Angelyn said it took over a year to arrange the financing for the mortgage. In 1994 she bought 38 expensive acres (15.37 ha) on Bowen Island. By 2000, when mortgage payments were five months in arrears, she would go to Opa and cry. She heard messages like, "Lean back on me completely. This is how strong you are. Just feel the weight of leaning fully back." In the meantime, telephone and electricity disconnection notices arrived. Angelyn was a widow with a young child to raise. She panicked. She felt terror. She had called everyone for help, tried to get more loans, all to no avail. A few days later she and a friend got on the telephone and acquired enough funds to put the mortgage back on track.

She appeared strong in character, perhaps strengthened by holding on to her convictions.

"The place has always had magic attached to it," she said, smiling with her round eyes. "There's something guiding the whole thing."

"How do others respond to Opa?" I asked.

Before the property gates were built, she said, she had met a couple at the entrance. They asked if they could continue to visit the tree—they had been doing it for 50 years. Angelyn decided to allow the public free access to Opa. She invited members of the community to build and freely use a small sanctuary in a meadow near the tree. They also helped to build a labyrinth; this too is open to the public.

"Many people have come here," she said. "We have worked with second phase recovery programs, for everyone from street kids to adults. They spend time with Opa. They go and hang out with Opa and get some of their greatest messages and inspirations."

"How do you get messages from a tree?" I asked.

"They appear in images, words, or full statements," she replied.

Angelyn invited me to a woman's retreat in June.

Four months later, we gathered in the large yurt at Xenia. We were four women, mostly from Vancouver, plus Angelyn. She explained the weekend protocol. The retreat would be held in silence. A vigil would be maintained in the sanctuary—at least one person must be there at all times; we were now a team with that one responsibility. Being small in number for a retreat, some Xenia staff would participate. There would be no sign-up sheet or schedule for the sanctuary shift. We could roam the property at any time, and would share that too with several horses, one dog and one pig. This was a place for relationship, I noted—conscious and subconscious.

In the silence of the first night, I sat alone inside the sanctuary, letting go of thinking. My attention went to Opa. When relieved by a member of the team, I went to lean on Opa's massive trunk. I imagined his massive roots below the ground, thinning out, becoming hair-like. I imagined how Opa linked to other trees underground. A fungal network of hair-like filaments attached to tree roots, helping them absorb nutrients. I visualized my legs sinking underground. What would that be like, I wondered, to be stuck in one place? So unlike my life experience. I could not relocate in search of somewhere better. I would have to adapt and accept what I could not change.

That night before sleeping, I could not find my toothbrush. In the morning, I asked a member of the staff for toothpicks and some salt; to do this I had to write a note. Later on, my wristwatch stopped. Small events asked me to accept. For a sense of time, I would pay attention to the quality of daylight.

Wandering through the meadow past Opa, I noticed foxglove growing on the edges of the woods. I recalled that Angelyn said she sprinkled foxglove seeds everywhere. That seemed appropriate for this place. The purple colour and tubular, fairy-like flowers on tall stems expressed joy and tenderness. Foxglove reminded me of the heart. I knew its chemicals were used as medicine for the heart; but in plant form, it was toxic or lethal if consumed.

I entered the sanctuary to replace a member of the team, and found my place on cushions scattered on the floor. I looked through a diamond shaped window in the front wall and beheld the forest. Mostly trees to look upon, and oneself to look inside.

Later on, we gathered in the yurt again to share what we encountered. Someone said that from the road, it looked like Opa had been topped. We spoke about our wounds. We were so shamed by them.

I returned to Opa. As I rubbed my fingers along the wounds, I noticed how well they had healed. We could learn from that, I thought. The healed wounds enhanced Opa's character. We could learn from that. We could be proud about our wounds. We could be proud how we responded. We could be proud that we persist.

I went to walk the labyrinth within another meadow, beyond a driftwood gate. A sign was posted that read: "This is a team event that awakens our intuitive ability to connect within a unique and simple framework of silence. It is a solo journey, yet one of cooperation, connection and communication. Dissolve the illusion of separation and find the One you've been looking for." The One? I puzzled. As I strolled along the spiral maze of pathways to the centre, it seemed like a metaphor for life. I recalled the story of Big Red—how a community was built by connecting to a tree, connecting land itself by connecting with the people. Was that the One, a network of all life?

I took my shift again and sat for what seemed to be a long time. I got hungry. Finally after dinner I was replaced. It was always the same person who replaced me, I noticed, and recalled the sign. We *are* connected.

Much later that night, I took my shift again. About 2 a.m., I was replaced. Tired, I went to sit on Opa's bench. As I sat, I began to feel a tenderness in my heart.

The next morning I found Opa in the same place. His massive trunk reflected morning sunlight, generating a warm yellow glow. I put my arms around the tree. As I did so, I felt my heart again, as though it opened up. I sat on one of Opa's basal bulges and leaned back. I sensed a kind of pulsing inside the tree. This being was like me, a host of cell networks that cooperated to fulfil a role, both within and outside ourselves, individually and in relationship.

I felt a light breeze, and opened to that too, allowing the breeze to blow through me. I looked upon the driftwood archway before the walkway like a portal. I felt gratitude for this place, and for a tree that welcomed me. I sensed how Opa stood his ground, adapting to what was dealt, be it axe or storms. Opa knew how to heal, how to bend, how to hold on. The more I leaned on Opa, the more I slowed inside. My heartbeat slowed, as did my breathing. I closed my eyes and waited.

Opa's wound

A deep peacefulness flooded me and I felt gratitude in my heart. I looked at features of this old tree, and what he gave: coolness by canopy shade, shelter for the animals, stable ground by holding earth in place, transformation of light, water and carbon dioxide into oxygen for us to breathe, building forest soil, and so much more we still don't know about. For all of this free life support, Opa asked for nothing in return, except to thrive. In this, we were the same: we seek to thrive, and we both turn toward the light. The more I leaned on Opa, the more I felt accepting toward all that I beheld—a bench, a group of trees, stumps and shrubs, ferns, spiders, foxglove, a horse neighing, a truck and its driver, an airplane and its passengers soaring overhead. And then I felt acceptance of myself. Being rootless did not matter. What mattered now was the new ground that I had found.

§◆

EPILOGUE

This book was written over a ten year period, beginning in 1998. The following updates were confirmed between April 2015 and May 2016.

Prologue
Although Clayoquot Sound was designated a UNESCO Biosphere Reserve in January 2000, and local First Nations purchased Clayoquot logging tenures, mining, logging and fish farming continue to threaten the ancient forests. The author of *Ecotopia*, Ernest Callenbach, died in 2012; Heyday Books reprinted the 40th anniversary edition of the book in 2014. Also deceased is ecoforester Merv Wilkinson, who died in 2011, ten years after receiving the Order of BC and the Order of Canada for his sustainable forestry work. He and his wife Anne were arrested during the 1993 Clayoquot protests.

Chapter One: The Askin' Rock Tree
The author requests information about the status of the Askin' Rock Tree from anyone who hikes into the Stein River Valley. Please email her at sharonmccann@telus.net.

Chapter Two: Luna
Stuart continues to monitor Luna. She is still growing—even growing bark over the chainsaw cut and metal hardware that supports her. In 2007 Pacific Lumber Company filed for bankruptcy protection, claiming that environmental regulations imposed by the State of California restricted the amount of timber it could log to make a profit. Mendocino Redwood Company, certified by the Forest Stewardship Council, assumed control of Pacific Lumber Company's timberland.

Chapter Three: Tree Keepers

Maynard Drawson died in 2012. In his honour, The Oregon Travel Experience, governed by the Oregon Travel Information Council, established the Maynard C. Drawson Memorial Award in 2015. The annual award honours individuals or group who champion Oregon's trees with the same fervour as Maynard. The winners are honoured at the Statewide Heritage tree dedication with a plaque, recognizing their contribution to Oregon history and heritage. The Pow Wow tree is in decline although still standing, with regrowth cabled to the main trunk and nutrients being fed to its roots through the asphalt. A seedling from the Pow Wow tree was planted on East Clackamas Avenue on public property to ensure its legacy lives on.

Chapter Four: Trees of Hope

Cathrine Sneed continues to direct The Garden Project, located beside the San Francisco County jail in San Bruno. Although jail residents no longer work on the farm land, it is used to train the city's at-risk youth, some of whose parents have been incarcerated. The Earth Stewards program continues to maintain city property. Anthony Travis was hired by the Public Utilities Commission and bought a home in the Bayview.

Chapter Five: Tree Oriented

When Vivian McLean died in 2011, she was honoured by many in Seattle as a visionary who worked without pay for decades as a community advocate. A memorial published by Crosscut.com noted that she had welcomed many people to meet beneath "a great walnut tree in a yard which is in some ways symbolic of the values she held. A greatness that survives over time." Vivian's property sold, and the black walnut tree still stands, being protected by its conservation easement. The Seattle Heritage Tree Committee approved 285 heritage trees in 2015.

Chapter Six: Forest Defenders

In 2006, a US District Court judge ordered that surveys continue for species at risk from logging public forest lands. Public land agencies continued to modify the legal requirement to survey, resulting in continued legal challenges by the environmental coalition. In 2010, the Clark timber sale was cancelled and the timber sale contract closed in 2014, 16 years after it was first approved. The old-growth forest defended by treesitters in the Fall Creek watershed was never logged. Cascadia Forest Defenders continue to protect old-growth forests elsewhere.

Chapter Seven: Big Tree Hunters
Ralf Kelman claimed to have nominated more trees than any BC big tree hunter in 2015, including the trees he co-nominated. Also in that year, more women had nominated trees—11 record trees and 3 champions. Maywell Wickheim died in 2015. His son assumed the responsibility to clear the trail to the Cheewhat Cedar after winter storms every year. Maywell never disclosed, not even to his son, the location of a giant western redcedar bigger than the Cheewhat that he had found. He photographed it, showed the photo to a few big tree hunters, and left it for his grandchildren to find.

Chapter Eight: Eagle Trees
The eagle cams set up in Kent, Ocean Shores and Puget Sound ceased to function. When an eagle nest was located in a 100-foot (30.5-m) tall Douglas-fir in North Puget Sound, WDFW set up a webcam. In 2014 the eagle nest housed two eaglets until they fledged and the nest collapsed from wear. Even the webcam cables were stripped, resulting in poor video quality. Eagle cam viewers could watch only pre-recorded videos in 2015.

Chapter Nine: Accountability Groves
Roaki travelled to California to test his hypothesis about physiological processes that define maximum tree height—this time with the world's tallest tree species, the coast redwood. He and his research team climbed the trees to collect leaves at varied heights in the tree. They discovered that tree-top leaves of coast redwood absorb moisture from fog and morning dew and store it inside the leaf so that they do not have to rely constantly on water supply from roots. This may be why redwoods can attain such great heights. The Wind River Canopy Crane Research Facility remains the only such facility in North America; 12 other canopy cranes operate on other continents.

Chapter Ten: Megamorphosis
In 2013, an old cottonwood estimated to be between 75 to 200 plus years received the title of Ashland Tree of the Year. It stood on city property, which the city wanted to sell for affordable housing. A condition of the sale was to cut down the tree to build up to 20 units. While the Tree Commission and residents protested, the city administrator declared the tree a hazard because it was dropping branches and fenced it. One thousand residents signed a petition to save the tree, concerned that old trees in Ashland were disappearing. In a 3-to-2 vote, the Planning Commission decided to deny the permit to cut down the tree. The city plans to sell the land parcel where the tree stands, and build fewer units for affordable housing.

Chapter Eleven: The Singing Forest

In 2011, Valhalla Wilderness Society proposed the protection of the Selkirk Mountain Caribou Park. It aims to connect the land between existing parks in the region to preserve forest biodiversity and habitat and for species at risk, such as the mountain caribou. Many endangered species inhabit the lower elevations of this mountainous area, which is the most economical to log. Ten conservation organizations supported the proposal, including the one Glada founded, the Applied Ecological Stewardship Council. The park proposal includes the Singing Forest— what's left of it.

Chapter Twelve: Dialogue Groves

Women continue to gather at the Women's Forest Sanctuary every summer. With much of the remaining old-growth forest in the Mattole Watershed now conserved, Sanctuary Forest continues to monitor conservation easements and promote stewardship and sustainable forest management. Hikes to Big Red continue as well.

Chapter Thirteen: Opa

Xenia Centre   celebrated its 20th anniversary in 2015. The Centre continues to attract people from around the world for creative, spiritual and wellness retreats, and to visit Opa.